AFRICAN CREEKS I'VE BEEN UP

By Ruthan Burchel

Copyright © 2007 by Ruthan Burchel

AFRICAN CREEKS I'VE BEEN UP
by Ruthan Burchel

Printed in the United States of America

ISBN 978-1-60266-070-0

All rights reserved solely by the author. The author guarantees all contents are original and do not infringe upon the legal rights of any other person or work. No part of this book may be reproduced in any form without the permission of the author. The views expressed in this book are not necessarily those of the publisher.

www.xulonpress.com

DEDICATION

To my only African-born son,

Jim

Known lovingly as 'Jamie" until he was seven years old

Truly Africa's best son

ACKNOWLEDGEMENTS

First and foremost to my beloved husband, Hal, who helped me remember some of the stories I had long forgotten and for his assistance with my farmer girl's grammar and spelling…

To my dear friend, and sister in the Lord, Sally Clark, for cleaning up my writings for me.. I love you, Sally!

*And, to all of you who think that a story was about you, well, maybe it was and maybe it wasn't! You'll never know…. There are many fish in my pond all over Africa….
Anyway, thanks for the story, if it was you.*

INTRODUCTION

It has been one of my dreams for years and years to write a book someday telling of some of the experiences I have had in Africa. I thought of the name for it, maybe fifty years ago. My mother often used the phrase, "Up a Creek Without a Paddle", and that is where I found the name, I guess.

The intent of the book is to let you feel many of the different emotions we, as missionaries, feel. I trust it will show you just how human we are. I have no intention of bringing honor to myself or my family.... but, instead, I want you to see how much God cares for each of us. He is constantly at work on our behalf. He has a great sense of humor and, I think, He knows just when we need to laugh, and provides us with something to laugh about.

I served first in Sierra Leone, West Africa, before our marriage. Then we were assigned to Zambia, south-central Africa. After our term of service there, we were in the States for fifteen years, mainly because I was not a teacher, and two of our children were coming into school age. To stay in Zambia, we would have had to send the children about 2,000 miles to school, and we did not feel God required that of us.

During those years in North Carolina a pastor came to our church who convinced us that every lay person had a responsibility to God to know how to lead another person to Jesus. This basic thought had never entered our hearts before, though we were both from pastor's homes. Hal became very involved in that program at church. It became a real passion for us.

When we returned to Africa we vowed personal witnessing would become part of our lives; and it did. Our problem was finding enough time to do it. This time we came to Kenya and a busy hospital. It was during that term we were sequestered to Samaritan's Purse to spend some time in Somalia.

Upon return to Africa after furlough, we were assigned to Tanzania. When the entire mission was banned from there, we thought our missionary career was finished. We retired and built a home in North Carolina, and settled down. Hal was working in emergency rooms, and I was trying to be happy as a full-time housewife.

Again, God spoke and we sold everything again, and returned to Kenya to the city to work with the people in the forsaken slums of Nairobi. We are doing no medicine now, only evangelism and discipleship. What a privilege!! We are seeing many people come to know our Lord. To Him be all glory and praise.

Read the book and enjoy.

TABLE OF CONTENTS

1. A Miracle, No Doubt 13
2. Bridges, or Lack Thereof 17
3. Ceremonies 23
4. Christmas in Africa 29
5. Enjoying the Journey 33
6. Flat Tires and Other Vehicle Problems 37
7. Game Park Fun 43
8. Hip-Spika Cast Saga 47
9. Hunger for the Gospel 51
10. Indy 500 Cow Race 57
11. Inventory Miracle 59
12. Jamie 63
13. Kilimanjaro or Bust 67
14. Kitchen Bloopers 73
15. Maina's Story 81
16. MK's 87
17. Matatus (the Public Transportation) 89
18. Medical Bits and Pieces 91
19. Mishaps or Near-Mishaps 99
20. Rookies 101
21. Saved to Be Saved 103
22. Snakes 105
23. Somalia in War Times 109
24. Sunday Afternoons 117
25. Sunday Evening Vespers 119
26. The Corset 121
27. The Operating Room 123
28. The Rooster 129
29. Well Baby Clinic 131
30. What Does It Take to Be a Missionary? 135

CHAPTER 1

A MIRACLE, NO DOUBT

We heard there was a new campsite near the city that had bathrooms like the ones at home. So we went to try it out for a couple of days. Those hot showers felt so good after a long morning of shopping for medicines and supplies! On our second day Hal took Jamie, our eighteen-month-old, and I took Martha, our five-year-old, and we headed for the showers. The building had two sides—men's and women's. In each bathroom there were toilets on one side, showers on the opposite side, and sinks at the far end. Hal had taken Jamie to the sinks to undress him, and the minute the last piece of clothing came off, Jamie, in typical boy fashion, made a beeline for the outside door. Hal looked up, and to his consternation, he saw a huge snake curled up in the doorway. Jamie headed straight for it.

You know how many things go through your mind in such a short time? At first glance, Hal thought it was a black mamba, the deadliest of snakes. One bite and the person would be gone in a matter of minutes. He thought, "Likely the snake will get both of us, but here goes." He made a mad dash for Jamie—keeping his eye on the snake. Just as Jamie reached him, Hal breathed a sigh of relief. It was not a mamba, but a cobra—and one had time to get help with a cobra bite. The snake was eye-level with Jamie and about six inches from his face, swaying back and forth. Hal grabbed Jamie by the arm and pulled him straight up and slowly backed away. This activity was accompanied by loud screams for help, which I heard in the next bathroom.

I ran out to see what the problem was and found Hal holding Jamie, who was crying. For only the second time in my life I saw Hal turn "father" instead of "doctor." Neither one of us could think of what to do for an instant. Other campers soon arrived, and we realized Jamie was rubbing his eyes as he cried. This cobra had spit into Jamie's eyes. One lady knew exactly what to do and ran for milk. We washed his eyes out thoroughly and then drove to the nearest hospital. Hal was sure he had not been bitten. In the emergency department he was examined from head to toe, and no bite was found. He had quit crying by then and was back to his normal happy self. His eyes were a little inflamed, but no real harm had come to him. We were given some eye drops, and we went back to the campsite none the worse for wear.

My mother and I had made a promise. We would always tell each other everything we knew about a situation so as not to get secondhand word of things. So when we returned to our home, I sat down and wrote her the whole story. I assured her over and over Jamie was fine and no harm had come to any of us.

A few weeks later my parents were visiting in the town near where I had grown up. They looked up a lady whom my father had led to the Lord years before. They had not seen her in about ten years, and I had not seen or heard from her in more than fifteen years. She had moved to another location and changed churches, so she did not even take any of our church's missionary periodicals. In fact, they had a difficult time finding her, but they just felt they needed to see her.

When they did find her, she was still serving the Lord, and they were so happy to meet each other again. There were many years of happenings to catch up on in one afternoon. Finally, she asked my parents, "Whatever happened to that little girl of yours?" Now this lady couldn't drive a car, so we always picked her up for church and dropped her off on our way home. She sat in the back seat with me, and that is all the contact I had with her. Mama told her I was all grown up now. She asked if I was married. "Yes, she is." She asked if I had children. "Yes, two." She asked where I was living. "Well, she is a missionary and lives in Africa with her family."

Then, she related her story: One night she was awakened from a sound sleep and God told her to pray for Ruthan Fisher (my maiden name) and her family. She jumped out of bed, knelt by the bed, and prayed a very simple prayer. When she was finished, she got back in bed and went to sleep again. But in the morning it was still so vivid in her mind that she went to the calendar and wrote my name down and the time it had occurred.

Mother pulled from her purse my letter detailing our "snake incident." She read it to the lady, they compared times, and they determined that with the time change it had been exactly the time as when Jamie had been spit at by the cobra in Africa. God is so good. He knows no time barriers. And the lady was faithful. We are convinced she is the reason Jim is alive today. We have never seen that lady since, but in heaven we will thank her for that prayer.

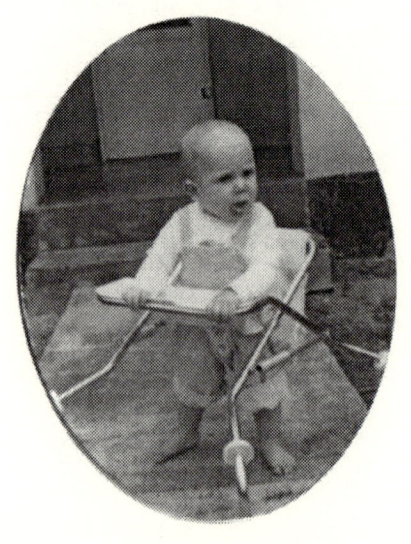

CHAPTER 2

BRIDGES...OR LACK THEREOF

I have been on all kinds of bridges! There are the nice cement ones you can meet a car on. There are the log ones where when one log is missing, you have to wait for them to cut down a tree and replace it. There are the little tiny ferries that are pulled across the river by ropes on pulleys. Then there are the big ferries that sandwich you in between them, forcing you to breathe a prayer that the weight is evenly distributed. And then there are the "no bridge at all" rivers to cross with a wench hooked up to the other side to pull you across. All bring their share of anxiety.

But let me tell you about one trip. We went on a monthly basis to a clinic that was staffed by a single nurse with a couple of helpers. It was way down in the valley, perhaps two thousand feet below our hospital and home. We usually went down one day, stayed the night, and came back the next day. We carried both medical and food supplies. One day we started in a not-too-reliable jeep. We had heard of a shortcut and welcomed it, as the regular way took about three torturous hours.

So we started to follow our directions to this shortcut. Beware of shortcuts! The road sort of disappeared and then the path disappeared, and we found ourselves in a big swamp. When I opened my door to see how deep the water was, it ran in the door! Well, we put it in four-wheel drive and reversed until we got onto more solid ground, and with much grumbling and complaining we returned home. It was nearing sunset and the vehicle had no lights, so that meant there was no way to continue driving. After arriving home, we discovered that my purse had fallen out of the jeep when I opened the door to check the water level. It had little money, but our passports and driver's licenses were in it, so this all resulted in more grumbling and nasty attitudes!

We slept the night in our own bed. In the morning we proceeded again, only not on the shortcut, but the regular dirt road. All was going well and we were almost there when we came to the top of the hill that led down to the river which usually had a cement one-way bridge. Looking down the hill, we realized there was no bridge at the bottom! It had washed away the night before in a tropical deluge. We would never have seen the impending disaster in the evening. And had we plunged in, all would have been lost, including our lives. Thank You, Jesus!

Men came from the other side, made a makeshift pulley with a wheelbarrow on a rope, and we sent things across the river load by load. Then it was our turn. Hal went first and the water was up to his shoulders. He lost his shoes, but he made it. Then they put Martha on their shoulders, and over she went. Then, with a big strong man on each side and water up to my chin, I went! I think they carried me part of the way because the current was very strong. We spent a couple of days and then found a place upstream where we could wade across to our waiting jeep. The water had receded a great deal. God is good all the time!

Two days after we returned home safe and sound, someone brought me the purse I thought was gone forever. In it was all the money and the papers, safe, though soaked. The only thing that was missing was a little make-up.

When will we ever learn God really does know what He is doing? Sounds a lot like Balaam's donkey, doesn't it?

****

Years later, I was responsible for taking teams to work on an orphanage that was being built. My philosophy has always been "work hard, then play hard." It was our custom to work for about two weeks and then take the team to a game park to see some of God's other creations.

It was necessary to cross a big river which had no bridge, but two big ferries crossed it continuously during the day. There usually was a long line of lorries (big trucks) waiting to cross. Sometimes these trucks would wait for two or three days for their turn to cross. But if a passenger car or van came along, they were given first priority. Our plans were all made for an early morning trip.

Two days before the scheduled trip we happened to buy a newspaper, and low and behold, one of the two ferries had gone down the day before! Twenty-something people had drowned or been eaten by critters in the water. The balance had not been correct on the ferry, but they went anyway. Now the dilemma. Should we go and take a chance on the other ferry, or take the long way around which involved a couple more hours? Should we tell our team? They really wanted to go to the game park very badly.

We waited until the morning—we were to leave at 6 a.m. We told our friends our plight, and all together we decided to take the long way. And we were glad we did, because later we discovered they had closed the other ferry down also, in order to dredge the river for bodies and debris. Thanks again, Jesus.

****

Shortly after the rains had finished, we went to the city to meet a team of college kids who would be staying with us for part of the summer to work. There were four boys and three girls. Our Land Cruiser would not hold all of us plus all the supplies we had purchased, so we put the boys on the train and the girls in the backseat of the vehicle. It was a long day's journey, even though we started very early. There was a shortcut that we took when it was dry, but it was through the deserted bush country. At times we would need to stop and cut the brush or trees out of the way. It was *really* just a jungle path, but it saved about four hours. So we decided to try it, even though we had not heard of anyone taking it that season.

It was an eight-hour trip at best, and we had come seven of those hours with very little problems. There were wet spots, but nothing that four-wheel drive couldn't handle. Then we came to a place where the bridge was gone, and there was a roaring river in front of us. It was nearing dark, and the thought of turning around and traveling another seven hours to shelter was revolting. Either way, it was dangerous! Soon a crowd of men gathered, and they encouraged us to cross. They told us another vehicle had come from the other way that morning, and with their help pushing and pulling, it had crossed the river. But that was the other way, and the bank going our way was quite steep. Finally, Hal decided we'd try it! We all crawled back in and he backed up to get a good head start. Down into the water we went as fast as we could! He kept it moving until we started up, and then no more! When we stopped, my elbow was within four inches of water. This was a big, high vehicle, a Toyota Land Cruiser. The intake pipe was high above the car, and it was a diesel, and we were in low four-wheel drive. But it stopped!

Hal crawled out his window, waded up to dry land, and hooked the winch onto a part of the cement from the bridge. About twenty men pushed while the winch pulled by remote control, and inch by inch we came up and out of the water. Within an hour we were arriving home, where nice warm showers and a good bed awaited us! The next morning, we met the boys at the train station. They had missed all the fun!

CHAPTER 3

CEREMONIES

Weddings are a great time of celebration in Africa. Everyone is invited to the ceremony and a big feast is held after the wedding. We missionaries were all invited to one such wedding of the daughter of an important church leader. Now, truth be told, this leader and some of the missionaries were at odds, or in other words, they simply did not like each other.

After the wedding, all the missionaries were led into a classroom for the feast. They brought us the regular rice in one bowl and another container with soup which had meat in it. We passed it around family-style and each took what we thought we could eat. As we ate, different parts of the cow started showing up in the poor cut of meat; a tail did, but then the one that took the cake was a piece of jaw bone. In the jaw bone were several teeth remaining. And in one of the teeth was a huge cavity, and inside the cavity was a big kernel of corn.

The lady teacher who had this particular piece of meat was horrified! Some of us thought it was funny, but not her. She ran from that classroom yelling bad things about the whole scene and nearly losing all she had eaten. It really was quite obvious why they had separated us from the rest of the guests, and I'm sure they were watching and got a good laugh out of the whole thing.

****

We had not been in Africa long when Hal was invited to play the piano for the first African wedding he had ever attended. He felt quite honored and insisted that he be there ahead of time. We arrived at an empty church, but he started to play the piano. What he didn't realize is that African weddings seldom start on time. You see, if the bride appears too anxious to get married, that is not proper. She must appear coy and shy, thus delaying the ceremony for as long as possible.

This particular time, she managed to be one and one half hours later than the stated time. Hal played everything he knew and some things he didn't know several times each. By the time the last of the family was arriving, a storm had come over the hills. There was no way to shut the windows at the church. The piano was sitting in front of an open window, and the church was decorated with flowers from all over the mission. There was a huge bouquet of zinnias from my garden, I think, as they were the only ones I ever saw on the mission station. Anyway, they were in a tall glass jar of some kind. When the wind started howling, zinnias, jar, and water all came right down on Hal's head. He was soaked, and so was the piano and floor. The keys started sticking badly, but he had to keep playing because the bride actually did arrive about that time.

Well, as I remember, it didn't go on immediately. The rain on the tin roof was so loud no one could hear anything, so the bridal party all sat down on the front seat and waited while Hal continued to play his repertoire again until the rain ceased, and then he finally got a break. He has never gone to an African wedding on time again!

****

Funerals are always a rather sad affair, but in Africa they are especially sad. In the *bush*, which is where we worked most of our missionary career, you seldom find the pacifying niceties which help minimize the sorrow a bit. No music, no flowers, no one dressed up, no casket, no elapsing of time to soften the blow, no kind words of a preacher. There is only the stern reality of death and burial with much wailing and loud crying. There is no embalming, so a funeral is held within a few hours of the death. There is no undertaker or funeral parlor to make it all appear lovely. There are not even lovely grassed cemeteries with beautiful marble stones. People are often buried in a field with high grass near their home.

So when a teacher's wife whom had been a patient of Hal's had died, the teacher came to Hal. He said he didn't want the traditional kind of funeral. Instead, he wanted to have a service in the church with singing, a sermon, and an open casket. Plans were set in motion. A simple wooden casket was made, but it all took time and could not be completed before the next day. He brought a nice dress for her to wear, and of course, it was our job to get it on her and play undertaker. We had no way to embalm, and we wouldn't have known how if we could! So we were a bit concerned about the length of time between her death and funeral and used plenty of good-smelling antiseptics.

When the time arrived, her casket was carried from the hospital up to the little church. People came from far around to see this new way of doing things. Then the African minister stood and announced that Dr. Burchel would come prepare the body for viewing as it might have moved or her mouth might have come open during the transit from the hospital. So, most embarrassed, Hal went to the front where her casket had been put up on a table, pried the top off, used a handkerchief to wipe her mouth and face, and adjusted her head and dress. Then he went to the piano to play for the singing. The pastor told the people how to march past the casket and take their last look at their friend before sitting down so we could have the service.

After all that, there were several congregational songs, prayers, speeches, and finally a sermon. There was no wailing or loud crying, and after the service several of the strong men carried her to the place that had been prepared for the remains. Everyone stood around while they filled the hole with dirt, but no one flung themselves on the grave as was customary in traditional ceremonies. Thus, we celebrated the first Christian funeral in that place.

****

In every new assignment we had, one of the first things we did was look for a reliable national friend who could help us. He had to be able to understand English well enough to hear what we said and yet know Swahili well enough to correct our cultural and verbal mistakes. This time we were looking for someone to train in simple laboratory skills. The second person we interviewed turned out to be just what we were looking for. There was only one problem. He had scored all A's during his high school years except for one failing grade in chemistry. We questioned him as to why this was. He explained that when he took the class there was no teacher and no textbook. Their only source of learning chemistry was to try to get notes from other people who had taken the subject the year before. Everyone needed to take the national boards and pass them, regardless of the circumstances in their school. Of course, he failed, as did the entire class. So that told us he was very capable of learning lab skills if given the proper chance and training. Enock worked out beautifully, and he became a trusted friend.

After about two years of doing clinics and evangelism in outlying villages, it was necessary for Hal to return to the States for a few weeks to work. While he was gone, our little staff continued the clinics as best we could. After all, if we were to continue to give any medical treatment to the group we were helping, there was no other choice. It was better than nothing, so we continued. My staff consisted of two young men, Enock and Ben, and any other volunteers who would help pass out the prescribed medicine.

When it was time for Hal to return to Africa, I wanted to go meet him at the airport. It was at least eighteen hours away. We stayed at a mission guest house halfway, but it was a long trip. Hal said I could come, but that I had to bring someone with me. He didn't want me alone on those long roads, especially the first day when it was all dirt and bush. So I asked Enock to come with me. He readily agreed, and we started out for the city. The trip was flawless. Our Land Cruiser worked perfectly, and we enjoyed our hours visiting as we drove.

As we were nearing the city, Enock became quiet. Finally, I glanced over and saw he was crying. I asked why, and this is the story I received: his father and mother had both died, and he, being the eldest son, was left responsible for a younger brother and two little sisters. He had managed to keep them in school by raising peanuts on the family farm. When he graduated he worked hard for two years and saved up two hundred dollars, which he was planning to use to go to the city and find a good job and live there. He had never been to the city before, but he had heard of its great opportunities. He'd gone back to the village farm one more time to tell his grandmother and sisters goodbye. When he arrived he found his grandmother ill and his sisters without proper clothes, with very little food left to eat, and with no money. It hurt to see them in such desperate poverty. He had trouble sleeping that night. In the morning, his decision had been made. He gave them his two hundred dollars, and he gave up the idea of going to the city.

He cried to think that he was here, not having to pay a penny, on his way into the city with me. I found him a room at the YMCA, and I turned in at the YWCA just a couple of streets away. He was overwhelmed at the wide streets, the stoplights—there were none outside the city—and all the people. Things were just too overwhelming to comprehend, so he cried.

We got Hal, and the airport was also such a beautiful experience for him. We then finished our shopping and headed home.

Shortly after that, Enock announced his plans for marriage. The girl turned out to be a very sweet person who seemed to be just the right fit for him. At his request, we helped him make his wedding very Christian, yet with traditional elements. Then he asked us if we would stand in as his parents. What a privilege! We assumed this involved just sitting in the right place at the wedding, but we were wrong. At the reception, Hal had to give a long speech in Swahili. He was totally taken aback, but with God's help he managed to muddle through, and all the guests seemed to understand. After we went to America, Enock moved to the city, where he is now manager of a bank. He is still a close friend and son in the Lord.

CHAPTER 4

CHRISTMAS IN AFRICA

Naturally, one of the hardest times for missionaries is the holiday season. The best part of Christmas is giving to others, and it is difficult to purchase anything when one lives miles and miles away from the city.

I remember one Christmas when our two younger sons were high schoolers. I had been to the city, but I just couldn't find anything the boys would like. Finally, as I was buying groceries to go back up country, I ran across some American cereals. They were expensive, but I knew the boys had not had anything like that for many months, so I purchased two boxes of cereal, one for each of them. I think it cost me about eight dollars a box. But when Christmas morning came and they opened that package, there were two happy boys! It's the little things in life that count!

Another time when Joe was a senior, he gave me one of the best Christmas presents I could ever remember. He had been home from school over a month for the holidays. Hal and I were working every day, so it could get a little boring for a kid at home alone. I will never forget that Christmas morning. After we were almost finished opening our few little presents for each other, he led us to the front porch. There was a huge crate full of kindling wood with a red bow on it. Now that doesn't sound too profound to you, but understand the situation.

We lived high in the mountains, so almost every evening we built a fire in the fireplace because evenings got very chilly. There was always plenty of big wood to burn, but it was hard to come by small stuff to start the fire. We both worked all day every day in the hospital, and we were tired. It was too cold to sit down and relax without a fire, and it was too much work to have to cut kindling to start the fire.

Joe had spent hours and hours of his boring time alone during the vacation time splitting and splintering wood. He stacked it all neatly in this big crate and it sat outside the front door, ready to start our fires. I think that box of little stuff lasted us more than six months! It takes some ingenuity and love to work that hard on a Christmas present for one's parents. Thank you again, Joe!

CHAPTER 5

ENJOYING THE JOURNEY

My first two trips to Africa were on freighter ships. The first trip took twelve days, and the second, which was my favorite trip of all, took thirty-two days. This kind of travel is not at all like a cruise ship. There are about six passenger cabins, allowing for twelve passengers. We were treated like royalty. We ate in a lovely dining room with the captain and shipmates, and we seldom, if ever, saw the workers, who stayed several floors down from us. In fact, our cabin was right beside the captain's, and he took a real liking to our daughter, Martha, who was two years old at the time. We ate three square meals a day, plus four round meals, and available snacks all the time. We did gain weight, which was not so good.

It was great fun to stand up high and watch them load the ship. Big cranes moved the cargo from the docks down into the hold. On the floor of the ship there were crates and crates of Brahma bulls. My first thought was: "Oh, no! They will smell." But they didn't really, except for days when the wind was in the wrong direction.

Hal stayed busy reading a huge tropical medicine textbook from cover to cover, painting, eating, and sleeping. I watched Martha mostly, but I also read a lot and enjoyed playing board games with the crew members. Martha and I also watched the dolphins trailing the ship. We took Martha's little tricycle with us, and she had great fun riding it all over the deck. We enjoyed the company of another missionary family and a single missionary guy.

Our gyroscope broke coming around Cuba, and the captain was quite nervous, as there was only a narrow strip of open water in which to sail. So when we reached Santa Domingo, we stayed there for two days to get the gyroscope fixed. We got off the ship and visited the city, which was very interesting. We had lots of fun with our single fellow because the pretty girls with flowers in their hair tried their best to nab him. He would get right between Hal and me and hold on for dear life. It probably was a good thing, as those lovely girls had intentions to nab him for sure.

We sailed another fourteen days without seeing land, and then the captain told us that at 2 a.m. we would pass a small island which was inhabited. So we all piled out of our warm beds to see the lights in the far distance. Then, in another seven days, we docked again.

Sailing around the southern tip of Africa was different. There are trade winds coming from two directions, and it can be very rough. We were told that at times they would have to drop anchor and unload some of the cargo. But our trip was not that bad. No one could eat for two days because the plates would not stay on the table, and it was very difficult to get food in our mouths. We felt like drunks wandering around the deck. None of us could stand alone. And the poor cattle; they bawled and cried as they bounced back and forth. The worst was trying to sleep. One could *not* lay still! There was no space big enough for us to sleep any other way than supine! After two nights of no sleep, we solved our problem. We piled all the pillows in one single bed with the rails up, laid on our sides until we could hardly breathe, and slept like babies. It was a neat experience. It took a while to get our land legs when we finally disembarked, but it was worth it! I wish I could do it again!

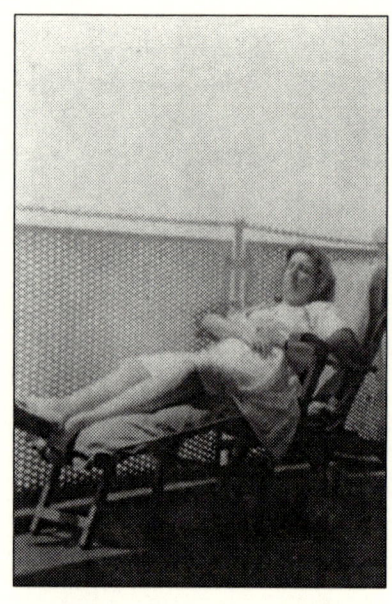

CHAPTER 6

FLAT TIRES AND OTHER VEHICLE PROBLEMS

Being a single missionary gal has it blessings and its trials. I can't think of any of the blessings right now, but having flat tires while you are the driver is no fun. It was one of the trials of my single life. My daddy was very faithful in teaching me how to fix one, but to have five on one trip to town is a bit much! One has to learn to not only take the tire off the top, but to change it, fix the old one so it is ready for the next flat, and put it back on top, secured into place.

My first trip away from the hospital was to take eight high school kids to a youth retreat for the evening. It was great fun. I was close to their age, so we joked and sang and had a great time all the way there and part of the way back. You don't know real darkness until you have been on a moonless African jungle road. That's where we were—on our way up a steep hill when we heard and felt the air go out of the back tire. I thought, "No problem, we'll just jack it up and change it. With these boys, I won't have to do anything but supervise." Think again! There was no jack to be found anywhere and we hadn't seen another vehicle since we had left the retreat. I was a bit anxious, to put it mildly. The kids said, "No problem! We'll just lift the car while you change the tire." I had never heard of it being done this way; in fact, I thought it was impossible. But they all scurried around and found big rocks to put behind the wheels, then loosened the lug nuts for me and handed me the spanner for when they lifted the car.

They all got in different spots and then someone yelled, "Hoist!" Everyone hoisted! "Hoist!" they yelled again. And everyone hoisted again and again. After five or six tries, I got the thing off. But that was the easy part! Now to get the crazy tire back on those bolts was a real challenge. But with the Lord's help and several more "hoists," we got the thing back on—all without a mishap! In another forty-five minutes we were back home—none the worse for the wear. A little missionary girl had learned a new life lesson in Africa.

****

When it was learned that I really was a farm gal and could drive and change a tire, I was elected to make many of the trips to the city for supplies. This was a long ten-hour trip with no pavement until the last twenty-five miles or so. I usually was given a helper to go with me, but still, I was the one calling all the shots.

I remember one time we had five flats in one trip! Who was dropping nails ahead of us? Anyway, the spare was on top of the vehicle, and huge—almost as big as a tractor tire. We would change the tire, cold-patch the one that had a flat, get that tube back in that crazy big tire, and hoist it back on top to await the next stop.

Another very necessary part of our equipment was a bucket. Often the vehicle would heat up, and we would have to stop and take the bucket to a nearby stream, fill it up, and carry it back to the car to fill the radiator and continue.

One time the radiator hose broke about fifty miles out of town. Now what? There were no stations close by, no AAA to call, and no cell phone to call them on! Well, I was praying for God to stimulate my creative juices when I came across three big rolls of bandages in the glove compartment. The women's' missionary societies had made them back home. They rolled them out of sheets torn in long strips.

Well, there was our answer. We pulled the hose together as best we could and then wrapped yards and yards of bandage around it as tightly as we could. It held! And we made it to town where we could get it replaced. Perhaps God sent a little angel to sit in there and hold it together for us.

****

Then there was the time we were following another missionary in her Peugeot to town to get the car repaired. We were probably going about forty-five mph. All of a sudden, her back tire flew off and went rolling into the ditch! We all made it to a complete stop without any accident. We saw the bolts had simply come loose. As usually happens, a crowd soon gathered to see what was going on. Hal gathered his wits, and offered a few shillings to anyone who would find the lost nuts. He thought if we could just find two or three, we could limp into town. But in five minutes flat they came with all five of them! I could have searched all day to find *one*. But then a shilling isn't as important to me as to the people who found the lug nuts. Soon we had the tire in place again and went to town.

****

Another time, four other single gals and I were coming home from some retreat in the late evening. It should have been about an hour's trip. There was no moon and no one else on the road. It was very narrow, and all of the hills were quite steep and curvy. We were doing pretty well until our lights all went out. Now what? We couldn't sleep here. It was useless to wait for another vehicle to come along, and it was way too dark to progress without lights. We could end up over the steep edge of the hill. We prayed, and then I, the youngest of the group, was elected to be the one to hold the torch. I propped myself up on the hood (called a "bonnet" in Africa) of the jeep and hung on for dear life with one hand while holding the torch in the other. God got us home just a little later than we had anticipated.

****

There was a missionary who was a real genius when it came to fixing a car. One time he was coming home when the fuel pump gave out. The landscape was quite mountainous. He was fine as long as he went down a slight incline, but as soon as he had to go up it would sputter and quit. So whenever it would start to sputter, he would turn around and go up the hill backwards! It worked like a charm. The fuel would flow freely from the tank to the engine, and when he got to the top he would turn around and go down forward, thus keeping the flow of fuel to the engine.

I don't recommend this on the interstate highway, but on dirt hills that have no steepness regulations, it worked well for him and got him home.

****

At another place we lived we had an old flatbed Ford truck. It was wonderful for carrying things around town or from the town to the building site. There were no inspections to be had, because many things did not work properly. But it ran. The motor was under the seats and the fuel tank was missing, so someone had rigged up a forty-gallon drum which sat on the front of the flatbed, with a garden hose going from it to the engine. It worked just fine as long as we kept it filled with gasoline. It's amazing what will work in a pinch!

****

In the early days when many African countries were just securing their independence, many of the law enforcement people had no education. They looked so proper in their new uniforms, and tried their best to enforce some laws, especially in the towns. One time we got stopped, and the policeman asked us in broken English if our "speed-o-meter" worked. Hal said, "I think so. Check it out for yourself," at which the policeman stuck his whole head in the window, looked at it, and replied, "It's Okay. Go get your car washed."

****

Another time a fellow missionary was picking up some medical supplies for us in the city. There was a gate and a guard there to monitor who came in and out of the medical stores. The missionary stopped, and the man in the sharp, starched uniform handed him the book to register his entrance. The missionary said to the man, "What's your name? How old are you? What village do you come from? What time did you come to work?" The watchman answered each question promptly, and the missionary wrote each of the answers in the book and handed it back to the man. He glanced at it, smiled, and thanked the missionary, who drove on in to pick up the medicines. The poor man could not read, nor did he have any idea of why or what people were to write in the sign-in book. He just was doing his job, and he was glad to have a job!

CHAPTER 7

GAME PARK FUN

I'm not talking about the kind of place you take children to ride the Ferris wheel and the bumper cars. I am talking about real African animal safaris. Now I don't want you to think that all missionaries ever do is have fun, but game parks are one of our great vacation destinations, and there have to be some perks with the trade.

One time we were staying in this neat little thatched roof hut at night and traveling throughout the park with an armed game guard in our jeep during the days. We brought our food with us. Someone prepared it for us and served us on china and linens under a pavilion just a few yards from our hut. It was a good life!

There were just a few little problems. There was no plumbing or electricity. There was a washbasin and a bucket of fresh water set up on our veranda to bathe with. Unknowingly, we left our toothbrushes and soap sitting on the stand and in the night the hyenas stole them. We had wondered at the gleeful sounds we heard on the little knoll just a few yards away from our hut!

Another evening Hal made his last trip to the outhouse for the evening. When he started to come back to the hut, there was an elephant grazing between him and our cottage! He didn't want to call for a draw to see whose territory this was, so he ended up sitting on the one-holer for over an hour until this big guy moved on.

Several days later as we were leaving the park and had no game guard with us. We were on our own. Out near the exit gate we came across several elephants grazing in the trees close to the road. Every time we would try to pass, they would lower their big heads, stare at us, and flap their humongous ears. We would back up and wait a little while; then try again to no effect. It took us a couple of extra hours to give them their space before we could leave in peace.

One time I asked a game warden how these animals knew where the boundaries of the park were, as there were no fences or sign posts. He explained, "If my parents and grandparents and great-grandparents had left and been shot, I would likely learn not to go that way again." Oh well.

One time a monkey jumped in the car window. Quicker than scat, he stole the whole sack of homemade cookies we were preparing to take to a sick lady. Then he proceeded to a perch in a tree hanging over the car and ate them while we stood helplessly looking up, watching him enjoy them.

Another time a zebra chewed the paint right off the side of the jeep because we would not feed him (or so we were told). Fortunately, the window was up.

Once, our poodle got into a fight with a nasty little monkey in our back yard. I don't know what started the fuss, but Rubble would bark and the monkey would shake the tree limb and hiss. This went on for a while, and finally the monkey threw a hunk of the papaya he was eating at Rubble and hit him! That ended the debate. Rubble brought the piece of fruit into the house and hid it under the coffee table. A souvenir?

CHAPTER 8

HIP-SPIKA CAST SAGA

There was a very sweet older widow who had taught high school English all her life. She and her husband had served as missionaries during their early years, and after his death she asked if she could be of any service on the mission field. She was sent to us to help with our new secondary school. She was a refreshing delight. Her sense of humor diffused many tense moments among five old nurses with whom she lived. We loved her dearly, as did all who knew her. She was very fond of her African English students, and they also loved her devotedly. One evening she was assisting at one of their parties and was playing Fruit Basket Upset with them. It's a game where everyone changes seats and there are not enough chairs. In the USA, this is called Musical Chairs.

Well, she was all involved in the game, but her bones were quite brittle compared to these agile teenagers, and when she and a student aimed for the same chair, guess who won? She landed on the floor and couldn't get up, partly because of her laughter and mostly because she broke her hip!

Soon a stretcher was brought and we got her to take some X-rays to prove the diagnosis everyone had already made. In those days—the early '60s—there was not a place in the entire country where surgery like this could be performed, so there was no choice but to get her to America. In a couple hours, plans had been made for a doctor to go with her, and she would fly as soon as tickets could be secured. Someone left for the city ten hours away to get these tickets, and we were to get a cast on her so she could travel as soon as possible.

To put that kind of cast on would require general anesthesia, and she had eaten just previous to the party, so that meant we had to wait until 2 a.m. Now, let me explain the cast that was used in those days. It went from the waist to the ankles, down both legs stretched out in a "v" formation. There was a metal rod between the two legs at the knees, and, of course, a hole around the buttocks for bed-pan services. They were not easy to put on, and they were even harder to negotiate for six to eight weeks.

At 2 a.m. all of the medical professionals gathered in the operating room for the procedure. I was assigned to pour the ether by mask. Good assignment! Now remember what this cast looks like. It started at the ankles. One person held each leg out straight at the proper V angle while the doctors wrapped wet cast rolls round each leg. The metal bar was put in place at the knees, but it got harder and harder. This lady was big. Not fat, just big; about five-foot-ten and broad in the shoulders. As the cast came up, they kept pulling her down in order to come clear around her tummy and back to her waist. I think I was chosen for the job because I had very long arms. As they pulled her down, I had to reach farther and farther down the table to keep the anesthesia coming! At the same time, two other people—one on each side of me—had to hold her by the arms and shoulders to keep her on the table while they were pulling her off the table to get the cast on.

I can't imagine how they did it in the States in those days, as I had never seen how they put one on there. Anyway, it took all eight of us sweating and tugging to get that cast into place! Remember, it was the middle of the night, we were all tired, and we got slap-happy. We laughed until we cried, and all at our dear friend's expense. If she had been awake, she would have been laughing also! We worked for three hours, and before dawn we were quite satisfied that she had a proper cast and was ready for shipment to the States.

That is only the beginning of the saga. As we were in the operating room, someone else was busily making an ambulance out of the secondary school Volkswagen van. He rigged it up with a bed and mattress in the back, and by about 8 a.m. we loaded her in for the ten-hour trip over roads with potholes the size of a small volcanic crater. By midnight, she and the assigned doctor were on the plane headed home. They had to buy three tickets for her, and the plane took out three seats and secured her stretcher in their place. Only one hitch: she wouldn't fit through the plane door! They had to hoist her on a lift up through the cargo compartment to the passenger cabin. They were kind enough to hang a curtain around her, and she rode quite comfortably with the assistance of her private doctor sitting nearby.

In Paris, their first stop, an ambulance had been ordered to meet them. However, they didn't seem to comprehend the size of this lady's cast, and you know the French vehicles. They are tiny, fuel-efficient things that look like Lego cars. When the plane landed, here came her ambulance, sirens blaring and lights flashing to meet her. They brought her down, but she would not fit in the ambulance. It was mid-January and cold. Finally, the best way they could find to transport her from one airport to the other was to put her in head first as far as the stretcher would go and then let her feet hang out the back door. They wrapped them in blankets, and there she went, flying through the middle of Paris with police escort and her legs hanging out the open back door. That turned some heads!

New York and Montreal were a bit better prepared, and she did not have to change airports, only airplanes. Her arrival in Seattle was uneventful, and by Tuesday morning she had had the proper surgery and a proper cast and started on the long road to recovery.

We felt proud we had gotten her to a good treatment facility in such an orderly and timely fashion. We all had a good laughter, and no one was worse off for lack of sleep.

CHAPTER 9

HUNGER FOR THE GOSPEL

One day Hal had been out about two hours, witnessing all day in small villages. A number of people had prayed for salvation. He was driving on a dirt path back to the main road toward home. He passed a little hut with an old lady sitting outside against a tree. There were chickens and children playing in the yard, and the thought came to him, "That lady is so old she likely will die soon, and I'm sure she has never heard the gospel." He had gone perhaps two miles past her, but could not get away from these thoughts. So he made a three-point turn in the road and went back to visit with her. Soon several other adults had gathered. He eventually presented the plan of salvation, which none of them had ever heard before, and fourteen people prayed for salvation. Hopefully we will meet some of them in heaven.

****

Another time, Hal had been witnessing in the slums in the city in which we were living. It had been a long day. It was getting late, and he decided this would be his last time to present for the day. He had been talking to a small group of young men who had prayed with him and had started to leave. A man in his late seventies had just walked up but had not been there long enough to hear the full plan of salvation—only the ending and prayer. Hal started to say his goodbyes when this man begged him to explain what they had been talking about. Hal was dead tired after about seven such encounters with small groups that day, and said he was too tired to do it again today, but he would be back the next Thursday. The man moved forward to look him straight in the eyes and said, "Do you want us to go to heaven...or hell?" What does one say to that? So he again explained the plan of salvation and another sixteen men prayed to receive Christ. Sometimes the flesh is weak, but the Spirit remains strong.

The workers are truly "few," especially in this kind of emotionally exhausting work.

****

While seeing outpatients in a hospital one day, a big, strapping Maasai with his beautiful red blanket robed across one shoulder stepped into the examination room. In a rather curt manner, he said, "I can't do what you told me to do!" Hal quickly scanned the man's record to understand what he was talking about, but saw nothing of pertinence. No diet to be followed, no exercises, nothing. So he apologized to the man and asked him to refresh his memory as to what it was he had been told. This was the explanation: "When you showed me the way to have peace with God, you read me a bunch of verses. You told me to tell all my friends about it, and I'm trying, but I can't remember the verses and I can't find them in the Bible you gave me! What do I do?"

Hal quickly sequestered the help of his nurse and I typed them out on a card with each reference. That was the man's prescription for the day. No charge!

****

In one city where we worked, there lived one million wretchedly poor people packed into one square mile of unbelievable conditions. There was little hope of them ever leaving the place. Many there were jobless (as are seventy-five percent of the people in that city), so there were always many men with little to do. Usually they are just anxious to talk or listen. This is where Hal goes on a weekly basis to witness. He just finds a couple of men talking, joins their conversation, and then introduces to them—many for the first time—the opportunity to have their sins forgiven and have a better life in eternity. Usually others gather and listen, and many pray for salvation.

One day a few ladies had gathered to listen, and one gal in particular prayed and seemed to really have the assurance of salvation. She was young and pretty and nicely dressed. She seemed a bit different than the others. After she prayed, she asked that Hal pray for her to find another job. She explained she was a bartender, and then Hal's African partner explained farther that she also was a prostitute. She begged them to go with her to her home to explain this newfound hope to her friends.

Reluctantly, they went with her to her one-room home and found three other young women there. They also prayed earnestly for salvation, and then they were on their way. The rows of shacks were so close that one had to straddle an open ditch in the middle of the path in order to walk. The ditch was full of trash, raw sewage, rainwater, and anything else that had found its way there. Just outside her doorway, Hal's foot slipped and his boot went into that sewage. The lady saw what happened and apologized, then ran for a bucket of water, got down on her hands and knees, and washed Hal's boot with her bare hands! Hal felt like Jesus must have felt when Mary washed His feet and dried them with her long hair. People who find Jesus are so grateful to the one who brings Him to them. Isn't this the place we would have found Jesus if He were still on this earth?

****

There was a road camp just down the hill from where we lived. There were perhaps one hundred men—some with wives and families—living there while they were building a new road. It occurred to us that they were all away from their homes and needed to know Jesus, so we made it our business to see that they heard. One evening each week, we would walk down and hold a little service with them. They seemed to really appreciate it. One week we had family visitors from the States. It was raining cats and dogs outside, and I decided not to go, but Hal went anyway. One of our visitors ventured out also, and rather than have a service, they just visited one little Quonset makeshift home to the next. At each home, Hal would present the gospel as they sat around on stools. Several people who were not Christians prayed to receive Jesus as their Savior. They did this in about eight or ten places and then came home.

Upon returning home, our visitor said with tears in his eyes, "Now I understand why you are in Africa!"

Yes, this is why we leave home, family, friends, and all the things that make us so comfortable in the USA and come to a foreign land. Jesus really does love all the people of the world! Not just us!

CHAPTER 10

INDY 500 COW RACE

Generally speaking, in Africa animals run loose with a small boy to watch them. After all, they were made before man, so they have just as much right to the land as we do. Right? Well, for us Westerners that sometimes develops into a problem. Like on the roads filled with cows and cars, or in the hospital filled with chickens and patients. You get the idea!

At that time, our dryer was a wire rigged between two poles. One day our neighbor, a single missionary lady who was teaching in the school, had hung her personal items out to dry before school started. Later in the morning a cow rambled past and got her two-foot-long horn caught in a bra strap. It scared her to death and off she went racing for the finish line. Of course, this was some sight to see by everyone who observed it, and as she passed people all over the compound, they took up the race to catch the poor creature and relieve her of her underwear. Besides, it would never fit her—she'd have to have had a four-holer. Soon she had about fifty people chasing her, including patients, their families, nurses, missionaries, teachers, and kids. It seemed like most everyone was chasing her! After a nice long chase and tons of laughter, she was corralled, and the piece of clothing was retrieved and given back to the poor embarrassed owner. Someone had even brought a camera, so there is still living proof to this day! Oh what fun!

CHAPTER 11

INVENTORY MIRACLE

Jon, our middle son, was visiting us with a friend of his while on summer break from college. Of course, they wanted to stay busy while we were at work, so they were given the overwhelming job of taking inventory of the medicines and supplies in the storeroom.

Understand, no particular person was assigned to work there, and loads and loads of supplies, sometimes containers full, would come and get pushed into this huge storeroom. It was in the basement of the maternity ward, and was probably at least thirty-five hundred square feet. There were good shelves, rows and rows of them, but it could have been a full-time job just to keep them organized and properly inventoried. But there was not enough personnel to assign a missionary to this task. So when any of us had a spare hour or so, we would go down there and work at a little piece of it. No one *really* knew what was there, or where it was! So it was a big mess, to put it mildly.

Jon and his friend were given this task. They worked diligently for about three weeks every day except for Sunday. It was not particularly a fun job, as there were no windows there and they were away from all other personnel. Each one of them had a legal pad on which they were writing the contents of their self-assigned shelves. They had divided them equally, written down each item on their side, and were planning to put it all in the computer. They had developed a simple system of sign-in/sign-out so it could be updated easily every so often.

It was Friday, and they were nearing completion of the initial inventory. We didn't know anything about it until Monday, but one of the boys had lost his handwritten list of his half of the supplies! They searched all day Saturday, and again on Monday morning. It was simply nowhere to be found. They were devastated! That was a half of three weeks' worth of work, and it meant they would have to do it all again. There really was not sufficient time for that, and yet one half of an inventory was no inventory at all!

Mid-morning on Monday, Jon finally came to tell us about it. His friend stayed in the basement searching the same places they had searched several times previously. Jon asked if we could have prayer and maybe God would show them where it was. So we gathered in a small circle with a couple other workers in the emergency department. We had one interpreter named Alice, but she was so slow we would have fired her months before if her prayers hadn't been so valuable. Hal asked Alice to pray. Her prayer went something like this: "Dear Father, You know where this pad of paper is. You know we need it, and we need it now! Thank You for helping them find it now. In Jesus' name. Amen." When we dropped hands in that little circle, Jon's friend was panting outside our door from running all the way up to the ER. He had it in his hand! He said it was lying in plain sight at the end of one of the aisles of shelves. They had looked there several times because it was in a very obvious place. To this day, both boys swear that an angel put it there while Alice was praying. What a faith-builder for college kids! Again, thank You, Jesus!

CHAPTER 12

JAMIE

Our oldest, Martha, was three and a half years old when Jamie was born. She had been allowed to go to the delivery room with us on different occasions. We would set her on the counter at the head of the table, and from her perch she would take in all of the happenings. You see, African women are very different during labor and delivery than their American counterparts. It is a time to be shared with family, and an African woman's mama, aunties, and grandmother all coach her through it. The helpers are very supportive, and there is no screaming or cursing near a delivery bed. Therefore, my feeling was if Martha could have this great image implanted in the back of her memory somewhere, when it came her turn, perhaps we would have allayed some of those fears which so many American ladies seem to have.

Thus, when it came my turn to go to the delivery room, Martha had it in her mind that she was going with me. Forget that one! I was making no promises to be an ideal patient, and I didn't want my daughter seeing her mother misbehave! So we insisted she must go to our neighbor's house for the night as we had planned all along. She was most upset, but she went.

At 2 a.m. I delivered a nice big boy called James Curtis. As was so often the case, I felt fine, so my husband drove me back up to our house and I relaxed in our own bed.

At the break of dawn, Martha was up. She was told she had a new baby brother. At that news she sprang out of the neighbor's house and ran all the way up to our house. She flew through the front door, and just as she got to the hall door Hal stepped out to meet her. Her first remark was, "Well, is he black or white?" She was pleased, as were we, to see a beautiful little fair-skinned baby brother fast asleep in his bed.

****

Jamie was my climber. At six months of age we finally graduated him to a twin bed because we couldn't keep him in the crib! He would climb over the rails, and then fall to his "near-death" on the cement floor. I'm sure he had several brain concussions, because he would turn pale as a ghost, vomit, and then come round!

Not only did he climb out of bed, he climbed into and onto everything. I had to hunt for him more than once, only to find him in the pots and pans under the stove or in a cupboard. He was a rather quiet child, so it was always done without fanfare. He would just disappear.

He started walking when he was ten months, and one day we found him straddled on top of an eight-foot ladder! It was a common occurrence to find him on top of the piano, or worse, on top of the old kerosene refrigerator. Now that can be a hot spot. The flue comes out the top, it gets quite warm, and it billows black smoke if touched the wrong way. Believe me, this boy was not without discipline, but he just loved to climb!

One of the worst incidents occurred one evening while we were having dinner with another missionary family who had a son two weeks younger than Jamie. We were talking and laughing when all of a sudden we realized the boys were gone. We followed their trail, which led to the two of them sitting on the floor in our bedroom. They had stacked chairs, boxes, stools, and whatever else was necessary to arrive at the top shelf of our closet. They had found a shoe box with some spare medicines in it. Now, they were sitting on the floor, each with a bottle in his hands, sharing. One had Librium and the other had Duccolax. It was quite obvious they had each had their share.

We had no ipecac, so two of the parents went to the kitchen to mix up a potion while the two of us each took a boy on our hip, facing their heads toward the bathtub, and ramming our fingers down their throats. Finally, the mixture of raw eggs, vinegar, and who knows what else arrived. Then we held them tightly, turned them up, and made them vomit some more. Many pills came up and they both survived without any harmful effects, except for two days of diarrhea.

We were with this same couple at their house another evening. Again, the boys came up missing and the search was on. All of a sudden, the boys came running and screaming out of the laundry room. There was a metal coat hanger hanging in Jamie's right eye! We panicked again! Fortunately, it was only hooked on the lower lid, and there were only a couple of drops of blood. He seemed to have no fear, and as he told his grandpa a couple years later after a fall in the driveway which had banged up his knee, "Oh, don't worry, Grandpa. Blood dries quickly!"

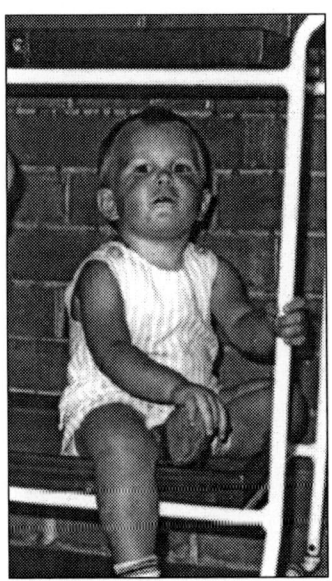

CHAPTER 13

KILIMANJARO OR BUST

We started out one bright morning. Hal, Martha, three single chaps from another mission, and I headed for the mountain in a big Austin. The guys had all paid their eighty dollars to climb, and Martha and I were to stay at the YMCA at the bottom of Kili while they climbed. I had carefully packed every morsel of food we were to eat on the journey, which was to be a three-day journey each way. For the most part, there were no restaurants, and gas stations were few and far between. So we carried all our food, an extra tank of gasoline, our camping and cooking equipment, plus personal belongs for six people. We had a packed car as you can see.

The first day was rather uneventful. It was Sunday, so after our noon meal we held a little service on the grass and took communion. It was very different out here in the desert.

We left home at 2 a.m. so as to reach the border by that evening, which we did shortly after dark. There we were held up over two hours. We had to totally unpack the car, and the customs officials looked into every bag and box we had. They were not on friendly terms with South Africa at the time and would not allow anything made in South Africa to come into their country. Most of our canned goods were made there. They tried to confiscate them, but we begged the officials to let us keep them because they were all we had to eat. Finally, they agreed to let us keep them if we took the papers off each can. So for the rest of the journey we never knew whether we would have peaches or beans when we opened a can for dinner! We had exactly the amount of money with us that we were allowed, so there was nothing to spare for a trip to the supermarket, even if there had been one.

We seemed to be off to a good start again until several of the places which were marked as "petrol stations" were either closed or out of gas. So we used up our extra tank and started praying in earnest. There were no other vehicles on the road, and it got mighty quiet in the car. At midnight we finally pulled into a tiny town and to a gas station, which was closed for the night. So we set up camp and slept the rest of the night. When someone came in the morning, he did have some gasoline and we filled up. There was only two-tenths of a gallon left in that tank. God was taking care of us.

Then we hit a stretch of washer-board road. I had never seen anything like it. The whole car jiggled so much you couldn't understand what other people were saying. Finally, the car broke down just a little after dark. Is it any wonder? Upon investigation, the battery had jumped off its moorings and hit the rotor, which had broken in two. No one goes anywhere without a rotor, I learned, and we didn't have an extra one! Sane people didn't travel after dark in Africa, so there was no one to catch a ride with to town. After much prayer and a lot of searching, I found some super glue. Then we cut a strip of adhesive tape from the first aid kit into a very thin strip. We glued the thing back together, wrapped tape around it, put the whole thing back, and waited for it to dry.

Now this was lion territory, so we didn't set up tents. Besides, it was dreadfully hot. Some stretched out right near the car and some of us stretched out in the car. Suddenly we heard a vehicle in the distance! It was a big lorry. He stopped, saw our dilemma, and could offer nothing more than to help carry some of us to town fifty miles away to try and get another rotor. We agreed and said we would follow him as soon as we felt it was dry enough to start the motor again. At about midnight we started the car. It ran like a top, so we headed into town.

There was only one hotel in town, so it didn't take long to find the other guys. They were sleeping in one big room. It had four or five single beds, but the dirty sheets were folded up under the beds. I have never, in all my years in Africa, been in a filthier place! Being the only woman, they gave me a bed, but I couldn't sleep on it—even in my sleeping bag. I was sure I could feel bed bugs or rats, so I finally just slept on the floor for a few hours. The bathrooms were nonexistent! There was a hole in the floor in the center room which was used for that purpose. There was a shower head, but no curtain or privacy whatsoever. I didn't really need a shower. After all, we had another full day of driving over dusty roads, so why clean up now? There were probably eight to ten rooms surrounding ours. The stairs went down from that room, so it was the only way out unless one jumped out the window. They didn't charge us for our visit as we didn't stay a whole night. There is always a bright side if one just looks for it!

Early in the morning we found a garage that was open and bought another rotor. The guys changed it, and to this very day that fixed up rotor is in my box of keepsakes. It got us to town, and we did not get attacked by lions!

We headed on another day trip to the town at the base of the mountain. At dusk we came in sight of Kilimanjaro. It just stuck straight up there out of the desert and seemed to reach heaven. Much of the time it was shrouded in clouds, but that night we got a peek at it, and it scared us!

We all got settled in at the YMCA, and the next day I drove them to their starting point and bid them farewell. Martha and I settled into a lovely little five-day vacation. There was a big veranda where we spent our days looking up at the mountain, wondering how their progress was going. On the fifth day we went to meet them. Hal was the first one down, and he reported that they had all made it. But some of their feet were in pitiful condition due to new climbing boots. Hal had just worn his good solid hospital shoes and he was fine, but tired. When we greeted each other, I gave him the word that I was pregnant with our long-anticipated second child. What a reunion. Everyone showered in my room and we were off to drive for a few hours before sleeping.

At bedtime we started to look for a good place to camp. Soon we saw this beautiful orange grove. It seemed there were no houses around, so we decided to set up camp there. By this time, we were pros at setting up and packing up camp. I was heating chili on our one-burner. Presently, we heard this noise in the distance. One of the guys stopped and asked if I had heard that. I confirmed that I had, and thought it sounded like a lion. The rest of our crew laughed at us and were sure a lion wouldn't be in this beautiful, tranquil spot. In a few minutes, the episode was repeated, only this time the growl was closer. Again, they laughed at us. I served the chili and everyone started eating enthusiastically. Then we heard it again, this time very close! There was no doubting its origin; it was a lion.

Usually it took almost an hour to pack the car. That night inside of five minutes everything and everyone was loaded in that old car, and we were off down the road. I remember I was just sort of lying on my tummy on top of everything, and couldn't lift my head without hitting the roof! I don't know where everyone else was, but we were all there somehow!

There was a small town about twenty miles on down the road, so we decided we would just stay in town somewhere. As we approached the town, there was a sign for a campground. We thought: *Oh, how fortunate.* We followed the sign, and sure enough, there was a grassy spot away from the center of town. We started to set up camp when a big man in a uniform came up and demanded money. We had no money. And despite all our sign language and begging, he would not let us stay there.

One of the guys went running off as we repacked, determined to find a place for us. His feet were so bruised and bloody from being barefoot. Just as we were leaving he ran back and motioned for us to follow him. He led us to a fenced-in place and assured us he had gotten proper permission for us to stay there. Again, we set up camp and dropped off to sleep. At daybreak, I was fixing our oatmeal (which we had every morning) when I realized we were between three five-story buildings. People were sticking their heads out of various windows to see what these gypsies were doing in their courtyard. Bill had explained our plight to the European owner of the big, fancy hotel, and he was the one who had granted us permission to sleep in that courtyard.

The next day was a very long one. You have to understand that all these roads were dirt, and the dust flew like a Texas dust storm. The big lorries and eighteen wheelers traveled together, so if one had trouble, they called on each other for help. Getting around a whole convoy of these is terrible and quite risky, as one cannot see because of the dust. A few miles down the road I began to feel nauseous. We had just passed a huge convoy, but Hal reluctantly pulled over so I could vomit. That felt better, and I assumed I was having morning sickness. About ten miles farther, the same thing happened. We passed the lorries, I got sick, there was much grumbling, and we pulled off to the side while the lorries all went flying by again. After about four such times, Hal let someone else drive. He told me to open the door and that he would hold me while I vomited out the door. That worked a couple times, and then I felt the diarrhea coming on. So we had to stop again. I made my way to the farthest cactus, hid behind it, and proceeded to let it fly from both ends. I felt a quick stick in my behind; Hal had snuck up on me and injected me with 5cc of Chloroquin and 2cc of Phenergan—malaria treatment. After he had realized I had a high fever, he had decided it was not all morning sickness. Back in the car, all I remember for the rest of the day was passing lorries. I was out like a light, and everyone was grateful. They even fixed their own lunch.

While I was out, they decided there would be no more sleeping in the open fields or in hotel courtyards. We were going to stop at some safe place where there would be no thieves or lions. What better place than a police station? Well, first of all, there had been no rain there in more than eighteen months and the sandy ground had turned to rock. We broke most of the tent pegs because it was very windy. We finally decided everyone would just sleep on the ground or in the car. What we didn't think about was the fact that where there is a police station, there is a jail. And inside the jail are prisoners, some of them drunk as skunks. All night long they hollered and sang "Amazing Grace" and banged on the metal bars with spoons—not too conducive to sleep!

While Hal and Martha were sleeping in the car, someone tried to break in without realizing there was already someone in it. They ran a country mile when Hal rose up and said, "Boo." I made Martha wear pajamas that had long sleeves and feet in them because there were so many mosquitoes. That morning, I counted fifty-four bites on her hand between the end of the sleeve and her fingertips! Needless to say, we were most grateful to see the sun come up. After a breakfast of oatmeal, we were on our way again.

Another long day, and we were almost home. We had about two hundred more miles to go, but we didn't have enough petrol to go on and everything was closed. It was long after dark. This night we stopped at a nice-looking hotel and asked the manager if we could just sleep in the parking lot. He agreed. We were so tired and just plopped on the ground to sleep. Our only problem that night was the night bellhop could hardly stand to see these white people out there sleeping on the hard ground. He came and woke us up four times to see if we were sleeping. He invited us to sleep on the lobby floor. We were too tired to get up, and besides, we had only enough money for gas this one more time. It had to last.

The next afternoon we arrived at our home with only seventeen cents between the six of us, but with a great feeling of accomplishment and satisfaction. We had made it!

CHAPTER 14

KITCHEN BLOOPERS

My friend and fellow missionary gave instructions to her house helper before she left for work one morning. She asked him to go buy a chicken, kill it, clean it, and cut it up so she could fry it for dinner that evening. Secondly, she asked him to clean the cupboards "real good." She explained that he should take everything out of them, put things on the table, wash the cupboards out with soap and water, and put all the contents back in just as it had been. No problem, right? Wrong!

When she returned for a quick lunch, to her amazement, a big skinny rooster was running around the kitchen awaiting his demise. Furthermore, the contents of the cupboards were on the table as she had directed, but her house helper had his pant legs rolled up and was standing on the countertop heaving buckets of water into the white painted wooden cupboard. Where did she go wrong? Communication is quite difficult with one hundred-plus years of cultural differences...

****

At our house, most every noon meal consisted of a meat patty, mashed potatoes, and a veggie. That is fine, but sooner or later one gets tired of mashed potatoes. Our cook came with brilliant references, but his repertoire was quite limited. One morning I asked him if he knew how to make potato salad. Though we did not speak the same language, he assured me he did know how to make it through smiles and nods. I left the ingredients I thought should go into it sitting on the counter.

When we came home for lunch we had our usual hamburgers, carrots, and potato salad. Only thing was, the potato salad was a great tossed salad with lettuce, tomatoes, and cucumbers *plus* mashed potatoes mixed in. That's different, but edible!

****

We had no television stations to watch, so our evening entertainment was videos. We tried very hard to limit them to one a week, so as to not run out of new material. This was the night to watch a video!

We finished our evening meal, and my dear husband cleared the table and rinsed the dishes so they would be easy for our worker to wash in the morning. Then we curled up in the living room to watch a favorite. It was about two hours long, and at the end, we noticed water coming in the front door. This was strange as it was the dry season. Suddenly it dawned on us; it was not coming in, but going out. As we started to trace the stream we realized Hal had forgotten to turn off the tap when he was rinsing the dishes. During those two hours, we had completely drained the 250-gallon water storage tank!

There was water everywhere! The kitchen was flooded, and so was every drawer in the sink unit of the cabinets. It had run into the pantry, and the dining room was next. We had just painted the cement floor with a lovely light grey glossy paint. The room was thirty-four feet long, and eight and a half feet wide—I had had a table made to fit that would seat fourteen people easily—and that entire floor was covered with water. The living room was also covered. Water was under the only carpet in the house, and water was running out the front door. The only reason it did not go into the bedrooms was because there were two steps between the bottom floor and that part of the house.

What a mess at ten o'clock at night! We called in the night watchman, and together we swept, scooped, and sopped up water for two hours. The carpet had to come out, as well as the padding underneath it. The paint in the dining room all peeled, and some of the contents of the kitchen and pantry had to be thrown away.

The only funny thing—and Hal didn't think it was too funny—was that our newly painted floor was slippery as ice! Hal skated all over it, and one time he fell flat on his face. He was sure he had broken a hip, but we were all laughing so hard at him that he finally decided he would get no sympathy from any of us. He just got up again and laughed with us as he continued sweeping water. Needless to say, when we finished we were exhausted and ready for bed. Thank God it was dry!

****

One time before our house became the mission guest house, we met a group of what we thought were wealthy Americans. They came to see our hospital and stay the night with us. As I was nervously trying to get a meal put together that was fit to serve such elite guests, they arrived from their last stop fifty miles away. Of course, they were not used to our dirt roads, and all felt dirty and grimy and ready for a bath.

At that precise moment, our yard boy was working in the flower beds near the side of the house. He hit a two-inch water line coming into the house with a sharp panga (a large African knife), cutting it plum in two! Water went everywhere, flooding the drive and the yard. Everywhere, that is, except for the one and only bathroom and the kitchen sink! There we had no water. Hal ran outside with pipe wrenches and tools to try to repair the PVC pipe. Of course, he got drenched. By the time he got it back together, he didn't look much like the dignified doctor these people had come to visit!

Besides losing all the dignity he ever had, the people had no water to wash with or to flush a toilet because all the water from the thousand-gallon tank had drained. It took several hours to fill again from the well. I finished dinner without any tap water, and we had a wonderful meal together. I came to find out these people were just ordinary folk who enjoyed a laugh as much as we did. They became very good friends of ours, and we enjoy spending time with to this very day.

When we finally were seated to eat, a runner from the hospital came to inform us there was a lady who needed a C-section right away. So Hal excused himself, ran to the hospital, and returned to the table in thirty-five minutes after having completed the procedure and delivered a lovely baby. This group saw true missionary living at its best. One must be flexible and able to laugh at the situation at hand, no matter what it is!

****

Speaking of that water tank—let me tell you another story about it. It was built up on a contraption of various materials—whatever we could get to make a platform fifteen feet in the air, just high enough to set two thousand-gallon water tanks on. Now water is very heavy, you know. But this is the only way we could get enough pressure to push the water into our houses and the hospital. It was located on the highest point of the mission, which was only a few yards from our house. The platform was made from some old railroad ties that we had collected somewhere.

One day a railroad tie broke, dropping one of the tanks down, bending pipes and breaking connections all over the place. Again, water was spurting and running in every direction. The missionary in charge was up high on the platform with ropes and pulleys, trying with all his might to fix the platform and return the tank to its position. My daddy, who was there visiting us, walked by the road about that minute. He stopped, sized up the situation, and then very slowly and deliberately said to the missionary, "Well, praise the Lord, Brother." The missionary had not thought of that moment as being a "praise moment," but my "seasoned in the faith" father had learned to give thanks in every situation!

****

Another time we took a team of nine to a distant, remote place to build a church. The closest place to buy a loaf of bread was two hours from there. One could buy Coke, cabbage, tomatoes, onions, and goat meat in that little town, and that was about it.

I was to be the chief cook and bottle-washer for this gang. We were situated in a teacher's house, the best in town, and it did have a bathroom and running water. Running water, now that's another story! The drain in the kitchen was clogged up and the water faucet had a bad leak and would not shut off. So Hal rigged up a stopper for it with a piece of inner tube, and we just had to run to the not-so-lovely bathroom to collect all our water.

I had figured out every menu and tried to take everything we would need for two weeks. This includes all our pots and pans, dishes, silverware, a four-burner propane cooker, a water filter, and food. For example, I took sixteen dozen eggs, cans and cans of stuff, pre-made pancake mix, tons of homemade cookies and brownies, twenty-five loaves of bread, and on and on. We fed twelve people three times a day. There was no refrigeration of any sort, so after a day the cooler served as a storage unit. I also took a food grinder to cope with the goat meat, which did help a great deal. There was no oven, so everything had to be made on the top of our little stove. It was a constant battle to keep the chickens out of the kitchen, but we couldn't shut the door; it was too hot, and we needed the ventilation.

The goat meat was something else. They would bring it to me early every morning in a big dishpan. It looked like they had literally cut the poor thing into a million pieces. There was no rhyme or reason to their meat cuts. There were miniscule pieces of bones through every inch of it, so it had to be handled slowly to get them all out. Muscle, fat, bones, and tendons—all were well mixed together. It took someone a couple of hours just to get it ready to go into the grinder. I always had one college girl from the team to help me, and one day as it was coming out of the grinder, she said, "That almost looks like good hamburger!" We had goat spaghetti, goat hamburgers, goat Mexican skillet, goat gravy, goat anything we could think of! We didn't tell the others, so most of the time they didn't know what they were eating. But they were working hard and didn't care to be picky.

The final day was coming, a Sunday. Frankly, I was tired of goat. I had seen cows roaming around, so I asked the man who brought my meat if they ever killed a cow. He said yes and that he would bring me some early Sunday morning.

I was thrilled and planned a nice beef roast with potatoes and carrots in a big canner pressure cooker. On Sunday morning after breakfast was over, everyone but me went to church. I waited and waited for my meat to come, and it didn't come! Finally, about forty-five minutes before it was time for them to return from church, I realized I had no meat for dinner. I quickly surveyed the food that was left. There wasn't much there, but there were three cans of spam. So I opened them, cut it up to try to look like beef cubes, put them all in the pot, and put the pressure on our dinner.

I sat down to read my Bible while waiting for the pressure to rise and paid little attention to it until it exploded! The top flew off. Fortunately, I was not in the kitchen. Broth blasted in every direction throughout the kitchen. What a mess! About that time, one of the girls came bursting in the door, smelling the aroma of dinner cooking. She flew into the kitchen and slid all the way across the floor of broth-coated linoleum and onto her hiney! What a sight! She did not seriously hurt herself, but she did have trouble getting to her feet because it was so slippery. I don't know how, but there was still ample food in that big pan to feed the hungry crowd. No one asked, "What is this?"

Our vehicles were not nearly as heavy coming home because we ate almost every morsel we took. But we had enough to cope with hungry builders who did a lovely job of putting up a little church for the community.

****

Water. It is a precious commodity one cannot live without. But in a third world country, one must be very careful with reference to where it comes from and how it is purified. Some often wonder why missionaries have house help. Well, water preparation is a good example of the answer to that question.

I have never lived in any place in Africa where it was not necessary to process the drinking water. Some places more processing is needed than in other places. In one place we had to collect the water from the faucet into a five-gallon bucket. There often were critters larger than bacteria and germs coming from the tap. To this bucket we would add powdered alum, and after it sat for twenty-four hours there would be two inches of solid material filtered out in the bottom of the bucket. The water was then skimmed off the top and boiled on the stove for ten minutes. After that, it was ready to go through the slow-dripping water filter. When it came through that process it was ready to cool and go into either bottles for the refrigerator or ice cube trays.

Now Americans are famous for their love of ice. No other country demands ice in everything, but that's the way we like it! We had many teams, some for two weeks, others for several months. We always had visitors, and there was no other place for them to stay in town. So in order to have ice, I had one freezer used for only ice. We would freeze it in trays, then empty the trays into plastic bags, and then store the bags of ice in the freezer. That was the only way we had enough ice cubes to go around most of the time.

That is just one example of why missionaries have house help. Veggies had to be fixed from scratch. There are few prepared mixes or packaged meats. If we ladies did all our own cooking preparation and all our own cleaning, we would have no time to do any missionary work. It really is a full-time job just to cook.

CHAPTER 15

MAINA'S STORY

There was a mission primary boarding school at one place where we served. Part of the students' learning experience was working two hours every day. I had a little girl assigned to me, and she would come every afternoon to do whatever I asked her to do. I guess she was about twelve.

One day she suddenly became pregnant. We all felt very sad, as this meant she must leave school. When the truth came out, the father of the baby she was carrying was the principal of the school. But nevertheless, she had to go, and that meant it was the end of her education. I liked her very much and told her if she wanted to work for me after the baby was born she could return.

A few months later, Maina returned with her tiny baby on her back and carrying her box of personal belongings. We had a storage room and a room in a little building in the backyard that housed Hal's office. We got her set up there with her baby, and she started working for us.

She was a great worker. She was always pleasant, understood enough English to get along fine, and had a beautiful attitude and Christian testimony. She was rather quiet most of the time. One day she said to me, "You must come to my village and tell my people about Jesus." I agreed that would be great. But, as with so many things that are not on the calendar, it just got postponed again and again. Every so often she would say to me, "Don't forget about my village. I will take you there."

We were within weeks of coming home when she asked me, "Are you coming to my village before you leave?" I assured her we would. Then I went to the boss man and told him this visit had to be in our plans. He grumbled a bit, but he finally said, "You get things ready and we will go this weekend." So Maina and I packed and prepared to go. It was probably forty miles from our house.

We started out down the main road, then turned off. Each road got narrower until we were simply following a path. Maina kept telling us, "It's not much farther!" Hal kept complaining that we must be lost. Finally, we came to a wide flay. A flay is like a swamp except you can't see any water, just marshy weeds. Maina directed us to a higher part of the flay about three times. She said, "My village is just across this part of the flay." In Africa, where most of the travel is done by foot, one never knows how far or close something is by road. But Hal got out and surveyed this flay. When he walked into it, he found it to be knee high and not solid on the bottom at all. When he came back, still not too happy to be there, he said, "We just can't make it! We'll have to go home."

I suggested, "Why don't we pray about it first?"

He replied, "If you want to pray, you go ahead and pray!"

I said a very simple prayer for wisdom and power to get across. Then Hal had to give God a chance to answer my prayer, so we unloaded the car, he backed up, and we watched as he gunned it and in seconds was on the other side. Amazing! We didn't even have four-wheel drive! So we all picked up our stuff and crossed by foot, then put it back in the car and drove on.

Sure enough, just a few yards away there was a clearing with about twenty little round huts in a circle. It was all so neatly swept and it looked like a picture out of *National Geographic*. It was beautiful. In the very middle of the circle were two chairs set up for us. I think they were probably the only two chairs in the village. They showed us to our seats and gathered around to look at us. They laughed and smiled, and the children touched our white skin and soft hair to see if it was real. We talked every word of the local language that we knew, and they were so thrilled that we could talk to them. It was a delightful and very welcoming experience.

We heard the old ladies tell the children to go catch a chicken. We knew what that meant! Soon Martha and Jamie joined them as they chased around the huts, and the howls of laughter and chicken squawks were truly refreshing. Eventually the kids won, and then the final pleas of the beast were heard. Before long, we could smell it cooking. In due time, they came to us with two metal bowls of rice and chicken. The forerunner was a little boy who brought us a pan of water to wash our hands. Of course, there was no silverware, so it was important to clean our hands. We had learned to eat rather gracefully with our hands, so we did. Everyone sat and watched us, and we could hear the chatter: "Look! They eat just like we do!" Certainly it was the first time most of the women and children had seen a white person.

It was late afternoon, and Hal told them we wanted to have a service. It was obvious they had no idea what a service was! Finally, after much urging, they all sat down around us. There were maybe one hundred people, and Hal told Maina and me to start a song time. We sang the simplest songs we knew, but it was a failure. No one knew them or even had any concept of how to carry a tune. We tried for ten or fifteen minutes and finally gave up. It was Hal's turn. He prayed, and again, no one knew to bow their heads or close their eyes. We were in virgin territory as far as the gospel was concerned!

Hal thought he couldn't go wrong with John 3:16, so he read it and started to talk about what it meant. It was worse than selling a snow plow to an Ethiopian man! They talked the same time he did. They walked around and did their own thing, some tried to listen, but it was so obvious he was barking up the wrong tree! They just didn't get it at all. He was a complete failure! After about half an hour, he gave up. As it was dark by this time, we asked to be excused for the night and proceeded to our hotel to sleep.

Now our hotel was on four wheels; it was a Peugeot station wagon. We cleared the back, and Hal and I crawled in. Martha was on the front seat and 23-month-old Jamie was on the floor board. We opened the windows for a cool breeze because it was quite hot. But remember where we were? Very close to that flay! And there were thousands of mosquitoes breeding there and biting people at night.

We couldn't take it, so up went the windows. Then we were smothered with four people breathing deeply!

The worst problem was our location. We had parked just behind some of the homes for the night. It was Friday night. In the center where we had been so warmly greeted, they had moved in some logs and made a fire. A big forty-five gallon drum had been rolled in and put on the fire. It had to simmer all night long, and it was the women's job to stir the brew and keep it at just the right temperature. It was like sleeping beside a girl's dorm at youth camp! They laughed and joked all night long. Every so often, we would hear one of them say, "Shhhh! The white man is sleeping!" Then someone would tell a joke and they would burst into laughter again.

We gave up sleeping and found a spot in the bush to use as a bathroom and did all the necessary things one does in the morning. Of course, the children had slept through it all and awoke as fresh as daisies! Hal admitted he had prayed most of the night for God to forgive him for his attitude and to please help him to get through to these people. We dressed and presented ourselves to our friends again. They brought us oranges and porridge to eat. It was good, and our spirits improved.

Hal eventually asked if we could have another meeting. They agreed, and were much more subdued than the night before. In time, everyone gathered round. We just forgot the singing. That was hopeless! Hal was praying desperately for God's help.

He said to them, "I see you are making beer." Without any guilt or compunction of conscience, they told him they made it every Friday night. He asked why they made it. They told him it was very good beer, and people from all around came to buy their beer and would give them a little money to go to town and buy sugar and cloth. Hal asked if everyone drank the beer. They replied, again without any guilt, "Oh, yes! It is very good."

Hal said, "What about the children?"

They soon told him, "Oh, no. Not until they get about so high." They measured with their hands about five feet tall. When the children reached that height, then it was okay to let them drink it.

Hal then asked them, "Well, how does beer make you feel?"

They all laughed and replied, "Good! Very good! You are happy and forget all your problems."

Hal asked if that lasted forever, then. They said, "Oh no! The next day the happiness is all gone until the next weekend."

That morning he had the undivided attention of everyone. They understood and were glad to share their experience with him. Then we were just quiet for a minute and he asked, "So why do you really drink? Besides to get money and feel good."

It became very quiet; everyone was thinking. Finally, the chief of the village—the oldest living man—spoke from the back of the circle. Slowly and deliberately, he said, "You see, we black people have a heaviness that we feel all our lives. When we drink beer, we are able to forget it for a while." That was the answer to prayer Hal had been asking for! He explained that white people had this same heaviness. And in our country many people drank beer to forget it, too. All were amazed!

Then he proceeded to tell them that this Jesus he had tried to tell them about the night before had the power to take away that heaviness forever! He could give us peace, and then it would not be necessary to drink beer to be happy. They listened intently. They were like clay in Hal's hands. He felt so responsible to make Jesus known to them! Hal is not a preacher, and he wished with all his might that one had been there to lead them into salvation. It had not really dawned on us at that point in our missionary career that anyone and everyone should be able to lead another person to Jesus. We felt so helpless!

After Hal had tried his best to teach them, he asked if there was anyone there who could read. The head man said very proudly, "Oh, yes! We sent one boy out to school for two years, and he can read!" He was as proud of that boy as if he had just graduated from Harvard! Hal asked the boy to come to him. He was about ten or twelve. Hal gave him a copy of the New Testament, opened it to John, and told the boy, "Now it is your responsibility to read this to your people. This will show them the way to get to heaven, and have peace here on this earth." We prayed and went to our temporary abode to get ready to leave.

When we drove out, I will never forget the scene we left behind. They had put that little boy up on the chairs where we had sat and he was reading loudly and very slowly from John. He read like a second grader would read, but everyone's eyes were glued to him and they didn't even stop to bid us farewell! Such hunger for God's Word we have seldom experienced!

We couldn't get back to that village now if we tried. We came home to the States as planned, but we never lost sight of those people. In fact, that probably was God's method of getting us involved in personal soul-winning. It is an overwhelming burden to have people ready to eat from your hand and not know how to feed them. We simply pray that God used that little boy and a Bible to lead them into His kingdom.

CHAPTER 16

MK'S

One of the biggest sacrifices of missionary living is not being near family. Therefore, an unwritten rule was made years ago which says that all missionary adults are either called "auntie" or "uncle" by missionary children. There were times when we met adults whom we couldn't quite identify until they said "Aunt Ruthan." That gave it away.

One little three-year-old neighbor used to come over to our house at dinnertime since her family often worked late at the hospital. She was just big enough to fit her chin over the edge of the table. It was obvious she had had strict orders not to ask for things. She would view the spread of food and simply say, "Oh, Aunt Ruthan! You are the best cook!" or "Your dinner sure does smell good, Aunt Ruthan!" or "I wish my momma would make something like that, Aunt Ruthan." We would simply smile and thank her for all the compliments. Finally, when we could not hide our laughter any longer, Hal would say, "Would you like some?" to which she always gave an affirmative response.

One time we were just returning to our mission station to pack up and to move to another location. We arrived at a high school graduation, and it was customary to have a big party for all the new graduates from our mission. At the end, there was a blessing of sorts. One of the graduates came to Hal asking him to do his blessing. He told Hal, "you were the one I wanted, but I didn't think you were going to be here." That meant a lot to Hal; he felt quite honored.

Another time we were coming home for lunch, and the men had the top off our septic tank and were emptying it. Our neighbor, a little four-year-old girl, was bent over watching the whole process. Hal called her and told her to be very careful because she could fall in there. Her reply was classic: "Don't worry, Uncle Hal, I can swim!"

Another time we had some big officials visiting the mission. The same little girl had a pair of scissors and was cutting grass beside the front walk with her mother's scissors. As they came by they spoke to her and asked her how her job was going. Her response was: "Well, if everyone would just leave me alone, I could get something done!" What an adorable neighbor we had! She kept us in stitches.

We had a little friend who was not allowed to eat sugar. One day another neighbor had made a birthday cake, and when she returned, the icing had been carefully licked off the entire cake! At first, she was angry, but after realizing who did it, she just re-iced the cake. The little tike was so grateful to his "auntie" for not telling on him. What are aunties for, anyway?

CHAPTER 17

MATATUS
(THE PUBLIC TRANSPORTATION)

The following all happened in the course of two weeks. The electrician was to stop by the house and pick up his pay for doing some work. When he didn't come at the appointed time my daughter called to see if there was a problem.

"Well, yes, there was a problem."
"Well, were you sick?"
"No, not exactly."
"Well, are you okay?"
"No, not exactly. I have an injury."
"So sorry. What happened?"
"I hurt my knee."
"How did you do that?"
"Well, the matatu I was riding in lost its steering wheel and we went in the ditch and I hit my knee."
"Oh, dear! Were other people injured?"
"Yes, but everyone is all right. I'll be there tomorrow to pick up my pay."

****

A few days later, when the house helper arrived, he said that he had gotten home very late the night before.

"Well, why did you get home late?"
"The matatu I was riding in had a problem."
"Really? What kind of problem?"
"It caught on fire."
"Oh, my! Was it a bad fire?"
"Well, the fire was in the engine at the front and we couldn't get our doors open."
"What did you do?"
"Well, the women all started screaming."
"What did the men do?"
"We tried to get out."
"Was the fire bad?"
"It burned up some people's clothes and things that they were carrying."
"How did you finally get out?"
"The driver put the fire out and opened the doors."
"Was anyone seriously hurt?"
"No, just a big delay…"

This is one of the reasons we seldom take public transportation in Africa. It is not exactly the most reliable form of transportation!

CHAPTER 18

MEDICAL BITS AND PIECES

One time Hal and I were fixing and enlarging a little house for a couple who was coming to help us in the mission work. I was the only woman on the job, and my job was to keep tools and supplies in the hands of the workmen. I was also supposed to keep things organized and in place so they could be found.

All of a sudden I saw fresh blood on things, and as I followed the trail, I found the origin was my toe. The feeling in my foot was lacking a bit, so I hadn't realized I had cut it on a sharp piece of metal. It was hot there, so I always wore flip-flops, which don't do much to protect bare feet from injury. About that time, Hal walked by and found me nursing my toe. He took a look at it and said, "Woman, you about cut your little toe off! You have to get some stitches! How many times have I told you to wear some decent shoes?"

Our house was about a mile or so from the worksite. As we jumped in the car, he told me to leave the door open and hold my dripping foot out the door so as not to bloody the car. So I did. We got home without incident, he put in a few stitches while holding my toe to my foot, he bandaged it, and we went back to work.

One week later, I took the stitches out before we went to work. By this time we were putting that same tin I had been cut on, on the roof. Hal was up there working to get the valleys water-proofed when it started to drizzle a bit. He hated the idea of quitting because he was almost finished, but the rain was enough to make the metal very slippery. All of a sudden he started sliding down the steep roof. He grabbed for anything to hold him back, and in the process, he cut his right index finger quite badly. He came down dripping blood, too. I said, "How many times have I told you to wear gloves on the job?"

We knew the procedure well by this time, so we jumped in the car again and I warned him to keep his hand out the window. At home, I proceeded to clean up the wound. Hal was a wonderful doctor; a much better doctor than patient. He winced and fussed the entire time. When I got ready to put in the local anesthesia, he sat right up to tell me exactly where to put it! "Over about half a centimeter. No, down a little! Slower! No, not that slow! Go ahead; I'll just hold my breath!" And on it went. It really got laughable. He had all the same detailed instructions on which suture to use, how far apart to put the stitches, and how tight to make them. After all, I had put in a lot of stitches before, but not on my own husband!

I finally got them in to his satisfaction, and then I prepared to put on the bandage. Now I had taught the class on bandaging to nurses, so I had a pretty good idea of how to do it. Again he made suggestions and expected me to follow them. He really saw no benefit in wrapping his whole hand, so he prevailed. He went back to work with a simple band-aid like covering, which didn't even cover the entire cut. Needless to say, it became infected, and he had a nasty-looking finger for two or three weeks before it healed! Most things he does better than me, but that time he should have listened to me and let me bandage it properly!

****

Our trees were not looking very healthy. We couldn't figure out why until we discovered our night watchman was digging up the roots to make medicine with them.

****

On another occasion my kitchen spices kept disappearing. I mean, how many months, or years, should a jar of rosemary last? I never did discover why I was always running out of things I seldom used. Years later, while talking to our missionary neighbors, I was told it was discovered after we left for America that my cook was also a medicine man and had been making his medicines from my spices!

****

Another missionary lady went into premature labor at about seven months. There was no turning her around, so I stayed with her in labor while my husband and her husband went to make an incubator. They got it finished just in time for a little three-pound baby girl.

It was the neatest incubator I had even seen. It was a wooden box with a foam mattress cut to size. It had glass on all sides, and on one side the glasses slid open so there was a way to care for her. The glass top was on hinges and was rigged with a light bulb to keep it warm inside. The problem was we only had electricity about a quarter of the time. So they fixed it so that when there was no electricity the bulb was lighted by a car battery under the incubator. A car radiator hose was hooked to the end of a teakettle on a little propane burner to keep it hot. The other end of the hose went through a hole in the glass to put warm moisture into the incubator. We also had a little oxygen tank. The whole contraption sat in front of the fireplace, which we kept burning all the time. Though it did not have all the modern day regulators, it worked quite well and God gave us the sense to keep everything regulated.

For two weeks a nurse, Hal, or I sat watching her around the clock. Every few minutes she would just quit breathing. Her little feet were purple from the thumping we had to do to keep her going. She never really cried at all. We force-fed her through an eye dropper because she didn't want to eat. So it was a full-time job to keep her alive.

Hal always took the night shift. One night almost two weeks into this routine, he could not keep her breathing! Finally, as he saw he was losing her, he decided he would give her a little adrenalin. He diluted about four times until he had a very minuscule amount of medicine and then injected her with it. She took off in high gear. She cried and screamed. He even moved her to another room as he was afraid she would wake her parents. She yelled at the top of her lungs for about two hours. But that was exactly what she needed. It opened up her little lungs like they had never been opened, and from that night on she started to eat, gain weight, and act like a good little lady. Before long she was out of our incubator and progressing like a normal child. She's fine today, thirty-something years later.

****

One time I counted how many babies I had raised on the oven door. All in all, there were thirteen. Many people think of Africa as hot, but it was not always so, especially to a newborn at night. The most important thing was to keep them warm, and if a mother was not available for one reason or another, I would take them home with me for the night, bundle them up tight, put them in a little basket or box, and set it on the oven door with the oven turned on the lowest setting. That method saved several babies. In the States we would just stick them under a heat lamp or in an incubator for a few days, but when one does not have those conveniences, you learn to make do. So we did just that: made do!

****

When the children were little the only time they had shoes on was when we went to church or went to town. They loved being barefooted. In fact, that was one of the trials of coming home and going to school—the teachers tried to make them wear shoes all the time.

I can't remember how it happened, but Jamie stubbed his big toe somehow. This went on for a couple of months. I'll never forget one time he was in the pantry, trying to climb up the shelves when a large can of peaches fell on the very toe that was already bandaged and so tender. The nail came out and we doctored it. It was difficult to get him to soak it, but he spent many hours in the bathtub trying to get it soaked in two inches of water (which was all we dared use).

Anyway, it finally got so bad that Hal decided we really needed to see a proper orthopedic/pediatric surgeon. So we packed up and headed toward South Africa, where there was adequate medical help.

After the long day's trip, we looked through the phone book and called someone to make an appointment. That night while dressing the poor little fellow's toe—which was all inflamed, swollen, and pussy—we realized there was a bone sticking out. Hal very carefully pulled on it, and it came right out! The next morning the toe looked one hundred percent better and was not nearly as red and irritated or as tender to the touch as it had been. The appointment wasn't for a couple days, and by the time it came around, the toe was healing so well it was obvious we didn't need to see anyone else. We think God touched that toe. All Jamie is missing is part of the bone in his left big toe. And we had a nice little vacation away from home!

****

Out of about seven nurses, I was the nurse who had extensive obstetrical experience, so I was usually called for any OB emergency. One day they brought in a lady who had delivered one twin in the village more than twenty-four hours previously, but she had not gone into labor for the second twin. She was also bleeding quite profusely. I examined her and I was sure the baby was alive—she simply needed a little labor to deliver that one before she lost more blood. So I simply injected her with pitocin. Her pains started immediately, and within minutes she had the second little twin without any problem.

The family and friends who had brought her thought I was a "miracle lady." They couldn't believe how that little shot brought that baby so quickly. It was a darling little girl, and they wanted to know my name, so I told them "Ya Fisher." So that is the baby's name: Ya Fisha, as they say.

****

One day we were doing a clinic in a remote village. It was raining, so the one schoolroom we were assigned to became registration, the doctor's office, the pharmacy, and the waiting room. Ideally, these three would have been in different rooms, but again, flexibility is the name of the game. So registration was at the only door, Hal took one corner to see the patients, I took the opposite corner to treat the patients, and all around the walls and middle sat the patients waiting to be seen.

Hal was talking in Swahili and trying to be discreet as he examined and talked to everyone. Suddenly, everyone grew mysteriously quiet, and when I looked up they were all staring at me. Then they broke out laughing hilariously. Hal had gotten his pronouns mixed up when talking to a man who had a venereal disease. He asked the man, "Have you laid with any woman except *my* wife?" There is a big difference between *my wife,* and *your wife.* That is the reason everyone was staring at me. So much for the man's privacy! Hal quickly apologized, and we went on with our clinic.

****

One day I was doing a clinic by myself. I had just come back from dinner when I heard a crowd of people coming up the hill wailing and crying very loudly. This was not an uncommon occurrence and usually happened when someone was dying or near death. I stepped to the door to assess the situation but could see no homemade stretcher or any sick person. About that time they fell at my feet continuing to cry loudly.

Finally, I discovered what they were telling me. "Sorry, your president has been killed!" It was the day John F. Kennedy had been shot. It struck me sort of funny. I didn't know him personally; in fact, I don't think I even voted for him. But they thought I would be devastated, thus they were mourning with me!

CHAPTER 19

MISHAPS OR NEAR-MISHAPS

Many of the places in which we have lived in Africa have been at a high elevation. Thus, it takes longer to cook and bake things. Another contributing factor is because the cattle live off what they can graze. Therefore, they are rather lean, and it is difficult to get the meat tender for that reason as well. I used a pressure cooker a great deal in order to get meat tender enough to enjoy.

One day I had been in the kitchen making meal preparations when my dear husband flew through the door. The pressure cooker was sitting on the stove without any fire under it. He quizzed me as to why it was as it was, and I told him I was waiting for the pressure to come down before opening it. Without hesitation or much forethought, he said while muttering under his breath, "Oh, it's cool, I'm sure."

Quick as scat, he took the top off. Or, I should say, he loosened the top and the top blew off! I had been cooking beans, and the beans erupted in every direction! Fortunately, Hal only got a couple minor burns, but we cleaned beans off of the top of the cupboards. There were very few left in the pan, but they were in the cabinets and covering both the floor and cciling! I tell you the truth, until the day we went to America I found beans everywhere and anywhere. I don't think my spouse ever touched another pressure cooker!

****

My parents were visiting us. Mother was enjoying the warm sun on our front veranda. She saw a three-year-old missionary boy walking past the porch carrying an open bucket of paint and a big paintbrush. My mama called to him and said, "Freddie! What are you going to paint today?"

He quickly answered, "My Daddy said his car needed painting, so I'm going to do it for him."

Mother thought quickly and said, "Perhaps, first you should ask him what color he wants it painted."

Freddie replied, "Oh, yeah!" He turned around to go consult his father about the color. Grandmas are so wise, aren't they?

****

I received a frantic call from my neighbor, who had not been in Africa but a few weeks. She begged me to come quickly and see what the children were doing! I ran, preparing myself for the worst. When I arrived in her backyard there were three children, two of mine and one of hers, playing blissfully with the tire swing. The problem was they had dragged a dead four-foot-long monitor lizard from God-knows-where and put him up in that tire swing. They were having a blast pushing him higher and higher. It was totally harmless, just a little gross to a new missionary!

CHAPTER 20

ROOKIES

It is not easy to be a rookie in any new job, but being a new missionary is exceptionally hard. First, many times this person has been in school for years preparing for this great calling. Secondly, they are not usually young people just finishing college. They are often church planters who have pastored successfully in the States, doctors who have had successful practices, or builders who have been construction engineers. Then, within a few hours of crossing the ocean, they are the rookie. There are so many things to learn: a totally new language to communicate, different-looking faces, a new culture, and all these older and wiser missionaries looking on.

One couple we had the privilege of mentoring had both been raised in the city, which was a distinct disadvantage. They soon became our dearest and best friends, but the first few weeks were full of learning experiences for them. She was devastated when she found an ant in her hundred-pound bag of sugar. She was not aware one could set it in the sun for a few minutes, and the ants would flee.

When she found a spider in her freshly boiled and filtered water, she threw away the entire five gallons of water. Oh, that precious water—and the propane it took to boil it!

It also took a while for her to learn to cover every sack of groceries carefully and make a quick beeline from the car to the back door, otherwise the pet monkey would jump down and take the whole loaf of bread right off the top of the sack!

I'll never forget the time we bought a turkey for Thanksgiving dinner—a live one! Then we had the job of killing it. What a fiasco for someone from the city who had never even killed a chicken! It was too emotionally hurtful for our friend to just put one foot on his neck and take one quick whack. No, he hung the turkey on the clothesline, turned his head so as not to see him get hurt, and swung the hatchet at the squawking beast. Needless to say, he missed more than he hit. Finally, Hal learned of his dilemma and went and killed the turkey for him.

We had to pass over a small stream that, when filled with rain, was a challenge to cross. It was straight down one hill and then straight up another. Our friend was driving with us to show us his new home when we came to the stream. It was high. He said, "Now there's only one way to get across this." And he revved up the engine and hit the stream full speed. The jeep quit right in the middle! So we all pulled off our shoes and pushed the jeep all the way up the hill. When it finally dried out a bit, the jeep started, and on we went.

Our friend decided to spruce up his house a bit by putting crown molding in the living room. He bought just enough to do the job. He called Hal to help him when he had only one piece left that was more than four feet long. He had cut and cut and cut and cut, but those angles got him every time! They started over and accomplished the task together.

CHAPTER 21

SAVED TO BE SAVED

It was mission conference day, so the staff at the hospital was down to bare bones. We were passing the front doors on our way to dinner when coming up the path was the local ambulance. It consisted of four men with poles on their shoulders and a filthy old sheet tied to each end of the pole. Lying curled up amongst these rags was a little old African lady with snow-white hair. She had traveled this way, courtesy of her sons and family, for more than thirty-six hours to find help.

Two days before, a thief had entered the hut where the family was sleeping at night. All had escaped except this old grandma who was unable to run, and the wicked men had slashed her from one side of her chest to the other. When they had stolen what they wanted, they left her for dead. Her family returned and lovingly put her in this makeshift gurney and walked for hours to get her to the only help available: the mission hospital.

The medical staff led them into the operating room where they laid her on the stretcher. If an African can be white as a ghost, she was! But she was alive, conscious, and displayed a big smile, showing a lack of teeth due to her age. When we gingerly pulled back the rags which were covering her, we discovered her chest lying wide open. One could look right into the chest cavity and see her heart beating. The lung on that side was totally collapsed, and we all were amazed to see her alive in such a condition.

Each of us took our position. Two of them tried to insert chest tubes, another started to clean the area, and my assignment was to get intravenous solutions started. Usually this was one of my areas of expertise, but this thin little lady had no blood left to even find a vein, let alone thread a needle into it. I breathed a prayer: "Oh, God, help me!"

Then it came clearly to my mind: This lady was kept alive all this time so she might hear the gospel! I looked into her eyes, which were very close to my face as I was bent over working on starting the IV. They were fixed on me. I quickly and quietly asked if she believed in God. She nodded an affirmative. I then asked her if she knew His Son. A totally puzzled look came over her face, and she said, "Who is He?"

I answered, "His name is Jesus. If you believe in Him, when you die He will take you to heaven to be with God."

Her attention was focused upon me, and her eyes said, "Can this be true?" It was obvious to all of us that she would not live much longer. She had no blood left, and yet she was living!

I said to her very slowly and clearly, "If you believe what I have told you, say His name after me. Jesus." Her eyes were full of questions, and it seemed an eternity before she answered. I repeated, "Jesus."

Haltingly, she whispered, "Je...s...us, Je...sus, Jesus!" She repeated that name several times, each time lower and slower. Then a broad, beautiful smile covered her face. Her eyes closed peacefully and she left that old body to be with Him in heaven.

There was no doubt in any of our minds who had kept her alive for all those long treacherous hours and why He had done so. One soul is worth the whole world to Him!

CHAPTER 22

SNAKES

At one eighteen month period of our missionary career we were without electricity. Therefore, we learned to make do with Coleman lanterns, candles, and kerosene lights. One evening we were both sitting at the dining room table writing letters by lamplight when we got a craving for some popcorn. Hal, being the gentleman that he was, got up and went to the adjoining kitchen to pop us some on the propane stove.

Just as he was retuning, I heard him at my back at the door between the dining room and the kitchen. He said, very slowly and deliberately, which is not at all consistent with his personality, "Ruthan, put your feet up to the bottom of the table...now." I sensed danger. I slowly lifted my bare feet. Curled under the chair I was sitting on was a small black mamba! Hal returned to the kitchen, got the broom, and killed him with the handle while I sat very quietly so as to not disturb it. Baby ones have just as deadly venom as larger ones. Thanks again, Jesus.

****

I respect snakes. I don't like them and I will be the last one to pick one up, but I have enough sense to kill them rationally. At one hospital where I was working, the nurses took the call and the doctors were called only if there was no way the nurse could handle the problem. Obviously, there were more nurses than doctors during that period.

One night I was on call and got a summons to the hospital, I can't remember what for. I had gone down, taken care of the emergency, and was coming back home. It was around 2 a.m.

It was just a dirt path, but it had a thorn-bush fence on each side. It was really very nice and quite picturesque. I was about halfway home when I met another creature on the path, and he was right in my way. There was no place to go around him, and he wasn't in the mood to hurry on across. I had no choice but to kill him before he killed me.

So, with the long metal end of my big umbrella, I aimed for his head. I hit it first time (good thing!) and just held on while he slithered round and round, hitting my legs with his tail. Finally, he gave up, and all was quiet. I had just killed a six-foot-long green mamba. If you read their history, they are one of the few snakes who are actually aggressive. But I won that match before he could chase me!

****

We had two pets: one was a little dog named Rubble, who I could write volumes about, and another was a big tabby cat, Pepper, who was a great hunter. The only problem I had with his hunting escapades was that he liked to bring his trophies into the house. Now our windows and doors stayed open all day, and most of the windows stayed open all night, too. The weather is beautiful with warm breezes and cool nights.

I must admit, our bedcover was neatly folded and stayed in the corner beside our bed more than it did on top of our bed. There was also an extra blanket there which I often pulled over onto the bed in the middle of the night when it got really chilly. Like I said, our bedroom windows stayed open day and night all year long.

Well, my helper was cleaning in our room while we were gone, and realized the bedcovers in the corner were moving. Upon investigation, he discovered a big snake, injured but alive, curled up in between the blankets! There was no one else home, so he said it was useless to yell. He knew he had to handle this one alone. So he came downstairs, found the broom, went back up, and discovered the snake had moved under the carpet. He killed him through the carpet and then pulled him out and took him outside.

Now, to the real quandary! How did he get there? The second floor has no outside entrance. After much discussion, we decided Pepper was the culprit. There was a fragrant moon-flower tree that hung over the porch roof, which was just under one of our bedroom windows. Upon further investigation, we found cute little footprints on that window sill. Apparently, Pepper had caught this fellow and dragged him up the tree onto the roof and into our window. Snakie-boy had found a nice warm blanket in which to nurse his injuries. Well, the window had to be shut, Pepper had been there begging to be let in for two nights. No way, Jose!

Today Hal is making a screen for that particular window, not to keep the mosquitoes out, but to keep the cat and his trophies out! Who knows what he'd bring in next? Could be worse, in my opinion.

****

I was on vacation in an upstairs apartment. The family staying in the basement apartment had a child who was coughing incessantly at night. There was some cough medicine in the apartment upstairs and his mama had a key, so she came up to get the medicine. When she opened the door, there was an adder lying in the door sill, as they so often do. She didn't see it and stepped on it, and it bit her on the ankle.

Her screaming awoke both her husband and me. We came running. Although she was usually a very calm person and a very proficient nurse, she lost it! She became another person, screaming and thrashing in every direction. It took both her husband and me to hold her down. I slashed the bite with a new razor blade, as that was the emergency treatment, then I wrapped it and headed for the nearest hospital. She was given anti-venom serum and an antibiotic injection. All was well, however, she had a very sore leg for weeks and weeks.

CHAPTER 23

SOMALIA IN WAR TIMES

One beautiful Sunday afternoon a representative of Samaritan's Purse showed up at our hospital. He requested that all the doctors and nurses meet him in the meeting room.

The marines had just gone into Somalia to try to bring peace, and he announced to us that their organization was also going in to bring medical care. He reminded us that they had sent many medical personnel to our hospital, and now was a time he needed our help. He said they had many volunteers from USA, but they really needed a doctor and a nurse from Africa who were familiar with tropical medicine to help the Americans get some clinics up and running. He said he would like a husband/wife team. He also said he did not want young people who had children they were responsible for, as it was so dangerous. That combination sort of boiled it down to Hal and me! We immediately volunteered.

A few extra shots and a little preparation and we were off. There were no commercial airlines running that direction, so we arrived at the airport early in the morning and caught the first plane headed for Mogadishu. It was a transport plane, and we sat on kegs of beer. And forgot the seatbelts!

It was a beautiful flight. Out one side of the plane we could see Mt. Kenya, and out the other side we could see Mt. Kilimanjaro. We had no mountains to cross, so we flew relatively low for three hours. We could clearly see the nothingness below us. All of a sudden, the azure Indian Ocean and the city appeared below us.

Our landing was uneventful. There was only a shell of a building for an airport and no one to check us, so we walked from the plane to our waiting vehicle. It transported us the four miles to the house which had been rented for the use of Samaritan's Purse. It was large—many bedrooms, wide halls, several little balconies and verandas, a flat roof, and eight armed guards stationed on that roof at all times for our protection. There was a tall wall with broken glass and barbed wire surrounding the house and a small yard with huge iron gates that were locked at all times. We could hear shooting most of the time, and sometimes it seemed very close. We felt like we had just entered a war zone, and indeed we had!

We were shown to our room and set about unpacking and organizing medicine for clinics to be established throughout the city. That evening we had a good orientation from an older missionary doctor who had served for many years in strictly Muslim countries. We were told all the do's and don'ts and what our routine would be. He said we were not to mention our faith in any way; we were simply here to do medical work and show God's love in doing that. He said the only exception to that rule was if someone asked us a specific question about our faith; then we could answer it straightforward and honestly. Hal and I were really disappointed, because our main objective in being there was to lead people to Christ! But we changed our prayers. "Lord, help someone to ask us the right question."

Two days later we were on our way to a clinic. These were held in the open air under a gas station covering, in a bombed-out theater, or anywhere it was deemed relatively safe. We were escorted there by the marines who sandwiched our three or four vehicles in between their Humvees and tanks. We planned to never stop until we reached our destination, because there were snipers in many high spots— aiming at anyone moving about. This was the first time in two years any of the general population had had access to medical treatment, and they came by the droves! Their gratitude was uninhibited, and the mothers would often fall to their knees and kiss our feet after we had treated their sick children.

Anyway, back to "two days later." Suddenly our vehicle came to a halt. My interpreter, who had been a medical student at the university before the war, was sitting in the front seat with the driver. He turned to me and asked, "Are any of you experts on your holy book? See, four years ago someone from Nigeria gave me one of them, and I had just finished reading that New Part when it was discovered and they took it from me. I have never been able to get another one. It was most interesting to me, what it said."

I gulped real big, knowing this was the "right question" we had been praying for! I said, "Well, no, we are not experts, as we have studied medicine. But my husband, here, has read it through forty-three times, so he knows pretty well what's in there!" Hal took over from there, and they set up a time very early in the morning for him to come to our bedroom to talk privately about it.

How do you witness to a Muslim? That is the question Hal struggled with for several hours before that early morning meeting. The answer finally came to him: just like you witness to anyone! So as they sat together alone on the tiny balcony outside our room, Hal explained the plan of salvation. Confession and repentance were no problem at all, because all good Muslims do this several times a day. But John 3:16 was a problem.

"Do I have to believe that Jesus is God's Son to have peace and know I am forgiven?" What a battle raged, almost visibly, in his very being!

The answer: "Yes, you must believe that!"

Finally, as though jumping off a high dive into deep water, Abdi said, "Okay. I will believe it!" Instantly, he lit up like a light bulb. The change was instantaneous. That sudden plunge gave him the peace for which he had longed most of his twenty years! Acceptance was no problem. He literally glowed that day and for many days to follow.

Another person on the team had brought some Bible study lessons for a new convert. Hal photocopied this thanks to our generator, as there was no electricity in any of this huge city, and gave him the first lesson. They agreed that he would return the lesson to our room the next morning at the same time. They would review his answers, and Hal would give him the next lesson.

This happened every day. One week later, he informed Hal he was going to bring a friend to see him. Hal supposed he wanted him to lead his friend to the Lord as well. When he came, the three of them sat on the bed, and after brief chit-chat, Hal started into the plan of salvation. This chap was not as fluent in English as Abdi was. Hal got through the *confess* and *repent* by being as clear and simple as possible. The lad said to Hal in rather broken English, "Wait, let me pray for you."

In his heart, Hal was a bit frustrated. After all, a soul-winner likes to make sure his convert-to-be understands every point before prayer. But he swallowed and said, "Okay." This was his prayer: "Thank You, God, that I have confessed my sins. Thank You, God, that I have repented of my sins. Thank You, God, that I have believed Jesus is God's Son and He died for me. Thank You, God, that I have received Jesus as my Lord."

Hal started to cry. He then realized Abdi, a one-week old Christian, had already led this boy to Jesus. Because of his poor use of English, the only way he knew how to express it was to go through the plan of salvation in the past tense. There was such rejoicing, not only in heaven, but in that bare bedroom with only a bed and three people who loved Jesus!

We then learned that every night after work people would gather secretly in Abdi's tiny room. He would teach them a lesson and grade it in the morning. They filled his little room every night to learn by candlelight. Someone else had brought a cassette player and some Bible stories in the local language. He let the children listen to this first, and then it was the adults' turn. He made everyone go home by midnight so he could prepare his lesson for the next day. No one was allowed to start the lesson themselves until they had prayed, saying they believed Jesus was God's Son and had come to die for them. Within a five week period, there had been twenty converts.

Sometimes we went out into the countryside for clinics. Again, we were not to stop or get out of the vehicle. However, we came across a small hut where several people were begging the vehicle to stop. There was a very sick old man inside, and they wanted us to give him medicine. Hal went in, checked the old man, and found he was dying! He appeared to have tuberculosis, pneumonia, and last-stage malnutrition. You name it, he likely had it! He was unable to move, but was grateful to Hal and Abdi for their care. Then Hal prayed for him very simply in Jesus' name. He then called back to the vehicle and I prepared some strong antibiotic and vitamins for him. When the two of them returned to the car, Abdi said, "Our God will heal him!" Then he proceeded to tell everyone about the old man and that "Our God will heal him!" We shuddered inwardly. What if God didn't heal him? He surely was dying right then.

One week later we returned through that village. Hal and I hesitated to even look that way. But to our amazement, the man was sitting outside the hut, waving both hands high in the air and smiling from ear to ear! Abdi was not surprised at all. Of course, our God had healed him!

Another time someone stole my walkie-talkie while I was passing out medicine. To me, it was a desperate situation. We had divided into two teams that day and we needed to stay in touch. We had to contact them since they had the vehicles.

We prayed together, and again Abdi said, "Our God will find it." After about fifteen minutes of searching through the village, Abdi returned with the head man shouting loudly, "Our God found it!" Some boy had taken it thinking it was a radio. I hate to think of that boy's punishment, but that entire village knew our God was the big One and could do anything!

Little groups of Christians continued to meet long after we left Somalia, though it was necessary to move from one place to another so as to maintain secrecy. Persecution came. Many were killed. Some of them had been workers with us and became believers after we were gone. Abdi and his family escaped the country in the luggage compartment of a bus, but his aspiration is still to return and tell more of his people about Jesus. It is deemed far too dangerous for any missionaries to return to that country presently, but God still has His ways of finding hungry hearts.

CHAPTER 24

SUNDAY AFTERNOONS

Sundays were always our loneliest days. Yesterday was no exception. We had been to many of the churches in this city, but none compare to our home church and pastor. We went, but got very little out of the music or the sermon. We were a little discouraged and longing for a good "uplift" like Sundays at home. Hal was scheduled to go to the slums in the afternoon and hand out Bibles to the first set of converts to finish section two of the discipleship classes. This means they had completed seventeen out of forty-two weeks of lessons. Naturally, the lessons get progressively harder, so we gave Bibles at this juncture because they really needed one to complete the next section. To tell you the truth, he did not want to go to the slums on a Sunday. That was our day! But after we came home from church he changed into his mud-walking boots, and off he went rather begrudgingly.

When he returned three hours later, he was in tears! Some of the guys had testified, and their teacher, a pastor, had preached. Hal said he preached better than Tony Campola! His subject was "Where is your God?" It was short, but so potent and encouraging. It was about the children of Israel who were in captivity and being challenged by the prophet. The guys were so happy and triumphant and determined to win the slums for Jesus. They couldn't wait for the evangelism conference, when they could learn how to witness to others. Hal had to speak a few minutes, and they literally pulled the Swahili out of him! He even prayed in Swahili with fluency!

They are currently meeting in a classroom of the school. It is a mud and stick structure with a mud floor. There are no windows or doors, just openings in the walls. There is no ceiling, just a few tins across the top. They have formed a church called Victory Church, and their goal is to win the slums for Jesus and stop AIDS by teaching abstinence to the children and young people. This is a core group of thirty-seven men who are on fire for the Lord. It is so encouraging! We recognized many as those we had witnessed to.

After the benediction, they brought in two Cokes. One for Hal, and one for the pastor. That about tore Hal up! But then they brought them each two dozen eggs! This was their thank you for bringing Jesus to them. Like the widow's mite, it was all they had. Hal just cried and cried. They needed that protein so badly, yet they wanted to give to show their love and appreciation. That meant more to him than a ton of gold or the best home.

Prayers are making this happen. We really are seeing a revival in these slums. Who knows what God will do if you keep praying and we keep working. He promises He is able to do more than we can ask or think. Can you try to imagine that? Please, keep up the good work and don't be discouraged if you don't know much about the people you are praying for. Just keep at it. Prayer changes things, and we are seeing it happen!

CHAPTER 25

SUNDAY EVENING VESPERS

Every Sunday evening we missionaries met together for fellowship. We just had all arrived at our neighbor's house when an ambulance call came. That meant Hal would have to leave and go for the patient. That could take ten minutes or three hours! So the men all decided to accompany him in the station wagon. We ladies did not lack something to talk about, and after a couple of hours the men came back. When they opened the front door, they threw in ahead of them a twelve-foot python, expecting us to all scream and holler. But we looked, saw it was dead, and sat there unimpressed. They had run over it with the car back and forth several times till it quit moving. Then they threw it in the car thinking they would have some fun with us gals. The joke kind of dissolved when the big baby started to wiggle! We just put our feet up while the three men hustled around, trying to remove the critter.

What goes around comes around!

****

Another evening, prayers were at my house. We had this new missionary who was such a cut-up none of us knew what to make of him. All of a sudden, he jumped up in the middle of a song and started dancing around and yelling. We all just sat there stunned until we finally caught on that he had a biting ant up his trouser leg. He wasn't joking! A trip to the back bedroom eliminated the problem.

****

We always had some goodies to eat after we had fellowshipped a while. Again, the guys got called out to the hospital and left two of us wives to finish the homemade ice cream. We made it, put it in the freezer with all the ice we had, and started to turn the crank. At the same time, we yakked and yakked. It never occurred to us it was taking an extra long time (about an hour and a half) until the men returned. It still was not finished. What was wrong with this stuff? The men soon saw the problem. We were both left-handed and we had been taking turns turning the crank backwards!

When we opened our prized ice cream it was yucky butter. And all that ice was wasted.

CHAPTER 26

THE CORSET

It was customary to have a yard sale when a missionary was coming to the States for furlough. After clothing has been through hot weather, hot enough to put mold on your shoes in the closet, it really is of little use in the USA. The clothing had also taken several years of beatings, because this was the days when the washing was done with a big stick on a large stone behind your house.

One of my dear friends was leaving in a few days for the States. She had her yard sale. It went very well, and she sold all her used clothing. That was Saturday.

You need to meet this dear lady to fully understand the picture. She was a tall, large—not fat—lady. She was an English teacher, and she fit the mold to a tee. She was always very proper, and she walked and talked as straight as an arrow. Most of us wore as little as was culturally acceptable, but this friend could not find it in her to be without a full array of hose and all the garments entailed to keep them up.

Her flight home was scheduled to leave on Tuesday; therefore, she had to leave on Monday to get her plane. There was another ritual to be observed. The Sunday before a missionary was to leave, they were always asked to come to the front of the church and say their farewells to the congregation. This was a large church, perhaps over six hundred people, and our friend was asked to come forward. She needed an interpreter, and upon arriving on the platform, she searched the congregation for her favorite retired pastor. She called his name, and he came forward from the very back of the church. He was a small short man, perhaps, 5'2" and not a pound over 110. As we awaited his arrival on the platform, we missionaries who were sitting on the front pews noticed our friend holding back the tears. She kept wiping her face as though to wipe away something from her mouth.

When the interpret-pastor came within view of all of us, we understood. It was not food she was wiping off her face, but a laugh, and the tears were not of sorrow but of hilarity. Pa Mono was coming down the center isle with the yard sale's best full-length corset on over his long, flowing African robe as though it were a suit coat. One problem: it was on backwards, so it appeared as though he had a double hump on his back. Due to his stature, it came to his knees! We nearly fell in the aisle laughing—under our breath, of course. No one else in the whole crowd saw anything funny. Our English teacher managed to get out a few teary goodbyes, though her face was beet-red.

Whoever said missionary life was boring?

CHAPTER 27

THE OPERATING ROOM

We were assigned to a small mission hospital where no doctor had been for several years. Consequently, the OR had been used as an extra storage area and things were in total disarray. In our first few weeks there, we concentrated on getting it up and running. One of the first big jobs after the cleanup was to get the sterilizer up and running. This was no small task, since it was a kerosene pressure affair and had to be pumped up manually for a good long time. Eventually it did work, however, and for several years it did a good job of sterilizing our operating room packs. I never did quite trust the old thing, though, and was always prepared for it blowing the ceiling out of the room. It never did.

There was a small room, perhaps four feet wide by six feet long, which had running water and a sink. So we labeled it our scrub room. Apparently it had been used as a lab at one time or another—as it was full of glass beakers, funnels, pipettes, and numerous other unnamable pieces.

Now I am not generally a sort of person who scares easily. I respect all animal life, but I am not afraid of snakes or spiders as many women are. I do go bananas at the least sighting of a rodent, big or small.

Now back to the scrub room. We were vigorously cleaning and sorting when a tiny little mouse popped out of nowhere. I lost all control. Before I knew what was happening, I was screaming at the top of my lungs and literally climbing the walls to get out of there. I reached the outside door in a matter of seconds, and to my amazement there were about fifty African employees, patients, and family members congregated to see what was going on with this crazy white woman. When they learned it was only a small mouse, it became the joke of the week to everyone, including my husband. I was mortified, first by the rodent and even more by losing any bit of dignity I ever had.

****

That small room holds several interesting memories. Several months later when the OR was up and running well, Hal went into that little room to scrub a major case. To his amazement, curled up in the middle of the scrub sink was a huge, long cobra snake. Needless to say, that delayed surgery for a few minutes until the creature was killed.

****

One day I went into the operating room to prepare for a case. We used a lovely stainless steel table on wheels for the setup table. We kept all three sterile packs that we had on a shelf. As I reached under to pull one out, I discovered the old cat had crawled in under the outside door and had delivered her litter of five kittens on top of one of the packs. Now tell me, was it still sterile?

****

In the middle of one night we got called down to help a lady with a huge bowel obstruction. Surgery was inevitable. I prepared the room, and they wheeled her in and put her on the operating table. Hal scrubbed her tummy and proceeded to drape her to begin the surgery. At that precise moment, one of the bulbs from the overhead florescent lights decided to loosen and fall directly onto the sterile field in a million pieces. Fortunately, no one was hurt. We had not opened her belly yet, and we had another pack to use after the light was replaced. This was Hal's first bowel obstruction, so I held the book in front of him as he operated so he could glance at it as needed. Finally, he closed her up, confident she would do well—that is, if she observed all the rules of post-op surgery. Two days later, he found her sitting out on the veranda eating a piece of hard corn on the cob! Do you think that was part of the post-op prescription? But she did survive!

****

Why do the interesting things always happen at night, especially when there is no electricity and you have no generator? Well, no generator except for the one that makes the lights on a vehicle bright. This particular night there was a lady who desperately needed a C-section. To wait till daylight meant certain death for her baby and likely for her also. So with the aid of torch lights and the car's high beams coming in the open windows and door, Hal performed the procedure and delivered a lovely baby and had a happy mother to tell the story.

****

Another time, a lady was having a very difficult labor and the baby would not turn on its own or with the help of a doctor. She had labored all day long. So to avoid another late-night episode, Hal decided we would go home, have a quick supper, and return to do a C-section before it got dark. Apparently, the family and lady overheard the plans, and as soon as we left, they loaded her on the back of a bicycle—no cushion or seat—and headed for the village. That's just what it took! When we returned to do the surgery, they informed us of her absence. Shortly thereafter she, her husband, and a fine baby came back on the same bicycle to show us their remedy for a "stuck baby."

****

And then there was Ba Simon (in English "Mr. Simon"). He had come to the hospital obviously quite sick, but with very vague complaints: a belly ache, fever, general aches and pains, etc. So we had admitted him and started treating him for malaria, which most everyone suffered from chronically. A couple days later, a runner came in the middle of the night to tell us that Ba Simon was on the floor writhing in pain. We quickly ran down to the hospital to find it so. Upon examination, Hal decided he had a strangulated inguinal hernia. This requires immediate repair—a bowel resection. So we prepared him for surgery. Fortunately, this time we did have electricity.

Up to that time, most of the surgeries we had done were with spinal anesthesia. This time we did the same, but when Hal made the first incision, cupfuls of blood poured onto the field. This is not the result of a strangulated hernia. Upon further questioning of the patient, we discovered he had forgotten to tell us he had fallen off of a horse the day before he came to the hospital. That changed the story completely! He had a ruptured spleen! That's a big surgery in anybody's book. But here we were, belly open, spinal anesthesia, blood everywhere, and a ruptured spleen. This called for prayer. Hal told Ba Simon it was likely he was dying, so he had better pray. We had never heard better repenting at any camp meeting. He prayed, and so did we.

The Bible school principal had been called to assist. He had worked as an OR tech during his years of schooling, thus he assisted on many big cases. I was to be the chief anesthetist and general flunky, getting the operating team anything they needed. This was our first big case.

I started to pour ether to put Ba Simon to sleep, but every time I would quit. Hal would check his level of consciousness by saying, "Ba Simon?" Ba Simon would answer, "Ba Docatela?" All the rest of us were about to be gassed to death, but we couldn't get Simon to sleep! This went on until he was semi-comatose—whether from the ether or loss of blood, no one knows. Hal proceeded to extend the incision all the way up to the man's sternum. It was a lost cause. There was no way we could stop the bleeding and get that spleen out.

We scooped up all the blood we could collect and put it back into him via IV. We had no blood bank or any way to type and cross-match him, so all we could do was try to give him his own blood back and keep the IV's running.

Hal ran a few huge stitches through his skin to hold him together. We then loaded him in the back of our Peugeot station wagon and headed for town four hours away! We were certain he would die any minute. I kept two IV's running as fast as they would go, and Hal drove...or maybe I should say flew!

When we arrived at the hospital, they could not believe our story. But they got some blood running, took him back to surgery, and we turned around and came home.

One week later, we got a call from the train station fifteen miles away. Ba Simon was there and needed a ride out to our hospital. We were astonished, but jumped in the car to go get him. We got to the station, and he was not there. No one seemed to know where he had gone. We searched all over the little town, but no Ba Simon. Finally, we started home. It was raining cats and dogs. It was such a hard rain that it was difficult to see the road. Halfway home, bent over holding his tummy was Ba Simon. He was soaked to the bone, but happy as a lark. He was well and headed home with us.

We kept him at the hospital for a couple of weeks to get his blood count back up and get some nutritious food into him. During that time, both of his wives came to tend to him. Both of them and a couple of their children all found Jesus as their Savior. It was one big, happy family. God is good, all the time!

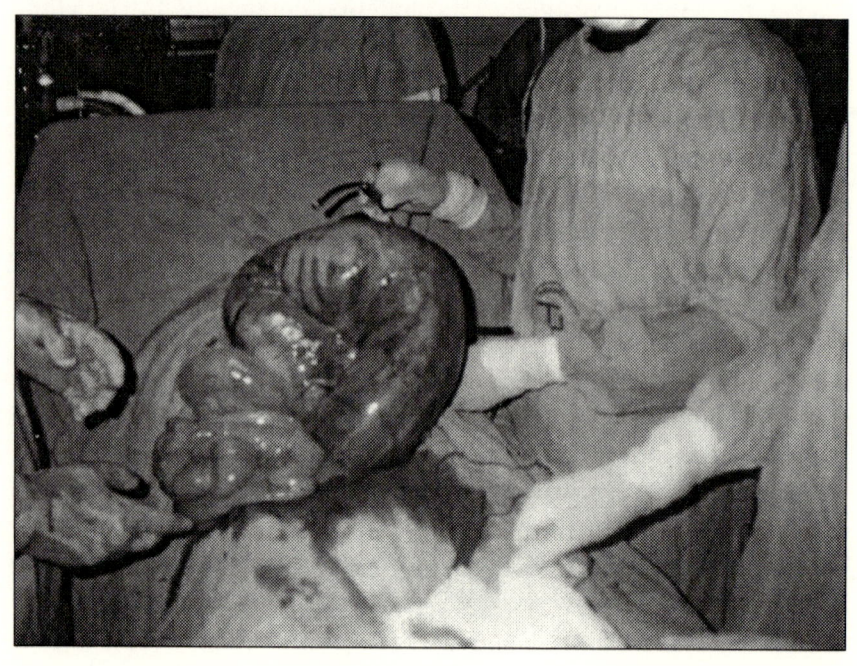

CHAPTER 28

THE ROOSTER

There was once a pet rooster named Peter. He belonged to our neighbors and best friends on a mission compound. My husband, Hal, did not have the same affection for him that we had for our dog and cat. They were very dear friends with whom we laughed and cried and played a lot of rook.

This pet chicken would roost in our poinsettia tree just outside our bedroom window. At 4:30 a.m. he would proclaim loudly it was time to rise and shine. His clock did not agree with ours, and it was annoying, to say the least. On several occasions Hal would throw a shoe out the window at him.

Finally, Hal would, at the first crow, routinely get up, go out, and put him carefully on his finger. He would walk him across the driveway to the fence and set him on it. Peter would go on crowing, but he was far enough away that he didn't awaken the whole household.

One day while coming home from the local church service, we saw Peter run across our backyard. Now Hal has very little sports ability and can't throw a ball straight. But when we spied Peter in our yard, he picked up a brick and slung it underhanded at Peter. Well, that big red fellow ran straight into it! Then he wobbled off into the banana grove. Hal felt a little twang of remorse as he had no idea he could hit the beast, so he spent a long time rustling through the banana leaves trying to locate Peter. He was nowhere to be found.

About the time dinner was ready Hal came in and told the family this was not to be mentioned to our neighbors. In a couple of days, one of them said to me, "We can't find Peter. Have you seen him?"

I replied, "Really? No, I haven't seen him either." All true, but not completely! About a week later Peter showed up! But he had a strange crook in his neck and every step was just a little sideways or weird.

In a few weeks, our friends were preparing to come to the States. They gave Peter to their house girl, who had married a Bible school teacher. She was aware of their feelings for Peter, and they thought she would take good care of him. On their last Sunday in the country they were invited to have dinner with Lazon and San Marie, their house girl and her husband. After a delicious meal, San Marie explained to them the most precious thing she could do for them was to cook Peter for their last meal! They felt like losing that last meal. And so was the demise of Peter, whom Hal had almost killed weeks earlier.

It was thirty-plus years later that we confessed our transgressions to our friends, and we all had a big tummy-jiggling laugh about it.

CHAPTER 29

WELL BABY CLINIC

Once a month we loaded up the station wagon/ambulance with immunizations and a couple of nurse's aids and headed out to a village to give vaccinations to all the children. We always took a Bible school student along to have a church service before we got started, as there were always many adults and children. There would often be a crowd of two hundred people, so that made for a good chapel service.

One day we stopped to pick up our preacher man, and they were all in exams. There was no one to go with us. Hal was not a preacher, but since no one else was available, he decided he could use the devotional he had presented to the workers at the hospital that morning. It was about Jesus casting seven demons out of Mary Magdalene.

Now let's get the picture: there were about two hundred women, a few men, and what seemed like a thousand crying babies all sitting on the ground in an orderly fashion. The nurses and I were seated in the front row of this church on the grass, and Hal and his interpreter were standing to give the lesson. A man named Simon was pacing behind Hal and mumbling under his breath.

Simon was a man in his late thirties who came periodically to the hospital and our homes to cut wood for our fireplaces and stoves. We all thought he was a little crazy, as he always mumbled under his breath and had an odd affect. He would cut wood several days, we would pay him, and he would disappear again for several weeks. He seemed harmless enough.

But on this day it was different. He never greeted anyone, he just paced back and forth within sight of everyone except Hal. His mumbling got increasingly louder and full of hatred. The reaction of the crowd was interesting to observe as well. The ladies all huddled their babies and children close to them, pulled their wraps up over their heads, and shrugged down as though trying to be invisible. A very oppressive atmosphere hovered over all of us. It was weird.

As I said, Hal was speaking about the demons being cast out of Mary. He told how one-third of the angels had been cast out of heaven with Satan, and thus two-thirds remained with God. Therefore, God's army was much more powerful than that of Satan, so we didn't need to fear Satan's power. Even though it was great, God's power was much greater, and He would fight for His children.

At this point, Simon was yelling loud enough that it was hard to hear Hal. We could tell he was yelling "no, no, no," but beyond that we could not understand him. Now Hal knew a fair amount of the local language, and suddenly he spun around on his heels and said in the local dialect, "In the name of Jesus, shut your mouth!" They stood for a few seconds glaring at each other, and then Simon turned and walked out of sight. We saw no more of him. The ladies relaxed, the wraps came down, and they straightened up and listened closely as Hal applied the lesson to their lives.

We immunized all the children present, and there was a free spirit of chatter as there always is when neighbors get together.

On the way home, the nurses were laughing and talking. We finally asked them what was so funny. They told us that Simon had been cursing us and God and had even said, "If what this man is saying is true and God is bigger, then let me be dead within a week."

Six days later, the word came that Simon had been found dead on the path. We were amazed and just a little frightened. The government was known for clamping down on witchcraft, but we surely did not wish to be known as foreign visitors who went around causing people to die. However, we discovered we were the only ones upset! Everyone else felt it a real victory for God and had fully expected it to happen. Why were we so shocked?

CHAPTER 30

WHAT DOES IT TAKE TO BE A MISSIONARY?

May I tell you my story? If the answer is no, just close the book. Otherwise, here goes...

I was born on a farm in northern Ohio in a non-dysfunctional family. My parents were very devoted Christians and loved missions and missionaries, though they never lived outside of Ohio until they were in their eighties. Looking back, I don't see myself as a rebellious child, but I did not plan to be different from the crowd! I loved sports and farm work and put my all into them. I was raised as an only child; my siblings were older, married, and away from home. Perhaps that made me love other kids even more. I constantly wanted to be with others my own age.

When I was eleven years old, I went with my parents to a revival service in another church in another town. I only knew one girl there, so I went to sit with her in the front seat. She was a few years older than me and was sitting in a full row of teenagers. We whispered and passed notes, and I did not remember one thing the preacher said. I couldn't even determine my state of grace at the time. I was simply a fun-loving kid. At the end of his sermon, he asked for those teens who would promise to live for Jesus to come forward. I had no feeling one way or the other, but when all the kids on both sides of me filed out both ways and I saw I would be left standing there, I didn't like that at all. So I followed them. The only place left at the altar was the very middle, right under the podium. So I knelt and closed my eyes respectfully as the preacher prayed.

Suddenly, I heard a voice say, "I want you to be a missionary nurse in Africa." I was stunned and thought, "Why is that preacher talking to me?" I looked up and realized he was not talking to me at all. Rather, he was just praying on and on about something else entirely. This had not even been a missionary service. I closed my eyes again, and again the same voice said, "I want you to be a missionary nurse in Africa." I began to cry. I had heard of people hearing from God, but it had never happened to me before, and I was in awe.

When service was finished, I went directly to our car. Eventually my parents finished talking to everyone. They sensed something was different, because I was always a social butterfly among other kids. They questioned me: "Is something wrong? Did you get into a fight with someone? Did you have your feelings hurt?" The answer to all these questions was no. And that was all I could say. I did not tell one person about that occurrence until I was fifteen years old.

I was headed down the wrong path because of my unwillingness to be different from the crowd, so by high school I was given the option of going away to a Christian boarding school. This suited me just fine. At a Christian boarding school I could be just like everyone else and still please my parents and God. I enjoyed most of my days there and did quite well, though I definitely still had my sins and faults.

At sixteen I fell in love with a classmate. I had many other friends—both girls and boys—but I was certain this was the one God had planned for me. I was prepared to wait until schooling was finished in preparation for missionary service in Africa. Graduation came and our paths parted, but we remained in contact with each other. I went to nursing school and loved it. But near the end of my nursing school days my "intended" married another girl and headed into a totally different vocation and direction.

I was heartbroken and absolutely certain that God had done this to me in order to make me an old maid missionary nurse. Well, I knew I would never be happy unless I fulfilled that calling, but I made a purposeful decision: if that was the way God wanted it, then

I would have my little fling first and discover for myself all the things I would be missing, then I would follow His calling for me.

And that's exactly what I did. I did it my way for two years, and it was more fun than you can imagine. But then came payday. And what a payday. I cried oceans of tears, felt like my life was ruined, and felt like I was totally rejected by everyone but God, who was too far away to care. Only fear of hell kept me from suicide on several occasions. I was so alone and disgraced, and you understand how that does not fit my personality.

Many times during these two years I heard from my true love—sometimes a phone call, sometimes in answer to the door bell, sometimes a gift from some faraway place. It made me mad, but at the same time I loved him and each of his attentions. I believed everything he told me and was certain if God had let me have him I could have changed all the things that were wrong with him, particularly his unwillingness to follow his call to Africa.

Finally, in the middle of my total brokenness and misery, I returned to the Savior and begged forgiveness. Shortly after that I had moved back home with my parents and was going with them to church. One Wednesday evening a young handsome guy sat just in front of me. I remembered him from camp meetings. We were never in the same group, as he was a devout Christian and I had been a very peripheral one. I was intent on not getting too spiritual, thus I had no time for him or his crowd.

But that night he looked a bit attractive. His socks matched his neat wool sweater, and I found out he was in college preparing to be a missionary doctor. I looked him over and thought to myself, "Well, now! He wouldn't make a bad second-best for me! I could live with that!"

That summer was full. I was working as second shift obstetrical supervisor in the local hospital and teaching the teens' youth class at church. I was independent and had a car and did many fun things with the youth group. He and I served as chaperones, and since I was a bit older than he, I became his big sister. When he went back to school we corresponded, and I was sure I had found my marriage partner. He was not so sure, and at Christmas break he broke up with me. Another heartbreak! This time I was mad at all men—except my Daddy, who could do no wrong.

I decided I had been good long enough to prove to the mission board I was ready to go to Africa, and I re-applied. By July I was in Africa. I loved it! I loved the people, the hospital, and the work. I was just glad to get on with life and, at least on the outside, to be done with all men. I worked hard. I was good at what I did and soon accumulated a lot of responsibility. I was tired and homesick most of the time, but happy to finally be doing what I was called to do: missionary work in Africa.

Six months before I was to come home, I was on vacation when I came across some people who knew my former first love. In fact, they knew him very well. I never told them about my relationship with him or my feelings for him, but as the evening progressed they told me of some of his capers and we laughed and laughed together at the ridiculousness of his egotistical ways and self-centered patterns. We had a great evening together. Then I went to bed. I tucked myself in the mosquito net and looked up toward the heavens. Through buckets of tears flowing down both sides of my face, I thanked God for saving me from such a trap. That very night I fell out of love with him, just as surely as I had fallen into love with him. It was such a refreshing release. I never did tell those people about us.

When my vacation was over I went back to our hospital to finish out my last six months of work. Of course, there was a stack of accumulated mail waiting for me. In that stack was a letter from him, querying me as to where I was, what was I doing in Africa, why had I deserted him, and several other pages of mushy-gushy stuff. He was planning to come to Africa in a month. He asked if I would meet him so we could have a great little rendezvous. I actually laughed right out loud. That was him, all right! I decided to answer, but I waited a week or so to do it.

In that same stack of mail was a very non-descript, generic Christmas card. It was signed, "As ever, Hal." Now, what does that mean? In it was a ten dollar bill, part of his tithe, I'm sure. No other note or letter.

Both of these pieces of mail were the very first correspondence I had received from any male friends in the two and a half years since I had been in Africa. I was quite taken aback. But I began to fall in love with Hal on the spot, and I haven't stopped yet. I am still falling!

After about two weeks I answered both of them the same evening. To Hal I simply said: "Thank you for the card and the tithe; I will use it to buy something I can keep." And to the other one, I wrote a lengthy letter explaining my feelings, the pain I had been through, and my new freedom from my love for him, and I told him not to be expecting me in town because I would not be there. I also proceeded to tell him that the man I intended to marry when I got back to the States would open the next letter he wrote to me. I had told him several times to "bug-out" of my life, but I think he always sensed I didn't mean it. This time, he knew I did, and I didn't hear from him in forty years. Then we met at a reunion, and I still felt absolutely nothing for him. Now only God can do that!

Hal's letters started coming regularly and got more and more intense, as did mine, and by the time I was ready to go home I was deeply in love with him, and he with me. Now if I had had it my way, I'd have been in a real mess. First, I would have married the wrong person, and that wouldn't have lasted any longer than his other marriages. Second, I would have married the right man, but at the wrong time. I was not ready for real commitment, and neither was he. I didn't love him then; I was still in love with number one. Only when God let me fall out of love with him could I fall in love with Hal.

I guess what I'm trying to say is God really does care for us, and He knows us well. He really does know exactly what is best for us to make us happy! He knows our future and wants only good for us! I hope that all youth could learn that lesson before learning it the hard way, as I had to do.

I arrived in New York City on the Fourth of July during the World's Fair. Hal met me at the airport and we were engaged that night. He drove me home, we announced our engagement to my family, and we were married six weeks later.

We set up housekeeping in Syracuse, New York, where he was in medical school. Eleven months later our first child, Martha, was born, and when she was two we headed back to Africa. We have been here now twenty-some years, with time out to school children in the States. We have Martha and three boys, Jim, Jon, and Joe. They are the delight of my life. We can truly say, "God is good all the time, and all the time God is good!"

Now you know what it takes to be a missionary. Nothing special. Not any special intelligence, not any great talents, no particular personality, not even super-spirituality. It simply takes an available person who is willing to totally commit to being and doing exactly what the Master wants us to be and do. If He calls you, you can do it!

Printed in the United States
201698BV00001B/211-1026/A

African Creeks
I'VE BEEN UP

RUTHAN BURCHEL is a career missionary nurse, housewife, and mother. While single she spent three years in a mission hospital in Sierra Leone. Since marriage to her doctor husband, Hal, they have served in several African countries including Zambia, Kenya, Tanzania and Somalia. Ruthan was born in Ohio, but after experiencing the great climate of East Africa without snow, sleet, and ice, they chose North Carolina as their home base. They have four children, all of whom love the Lord.

Ruthan's stated goal is to love her Jesus with all her heart and walk a consistent Christian life while enjoying the journey. Her dry humor works its way into most every day, as this book will illustrate.

African Creeks I've Been Up is just that! Here the author brings together a composite of every day experiences of a long-term career missionary. Some are hilarious. Some are quite serious. Some are miraculous. But the intent of all is to show accurately how diversified missionary life actually can be. It emphasizes the great need for a good sense of humor and flexibility – accepting things as they come our way, knowing that **all** *things work together for the good of those who love the Lord.*